W9-BPM-758

The Glory Walk

The Glory Walk

A MEMOIR

Cathryn E. Smith

VanderWyk & Burnham

Published by VanderWyk & Burnham
A Division of Publicom, Inc.
P.O. Box 2789, Acton, Massachusetts 01720

This book is available for quantity purchases. For information on bulk discounts, call (800) 789-7916 or write to Special Sales at the above address.

Library of Congress Cataloging-in-Publication Data
Smith, Cathryn E., 1957–
    The glory walk / Cathryn E. Smith
      p. cm.
    Includes bibliographic references.
    ISBN 1-889242-17-9
    1. Smith, Cathryn E., 1957– —Family relationships. 2. English teachers—United States—Biography. 3. Alzheimer's disease—Patients—Biography. 4. Fathers and daughters—United States. I. Title

PE64.S65 A3 2003
362.1'96831'092—dc21
[B]   2002035027

Interior book design by Publicom, Inc.

FIRST PRINTING
Manufactured in the United States of America
10 9 8 7 6 5 4 3 2 1

In memory of my father

Robert D. Smith

Tell me about despair, yours, and I will tell you mine.
Meanwhile, the world goes on. . . .

Mary Oliver, "Wild Geese"

CONTENTS

Introduction

> It is true that we can't take anything with us when we die; but that
> wholeness of our life, which we complete in the very moment of
> our death, lies *outside* the grave and outside the grave it *remains*—
> and it does so, not *although*, but *because* it has slipped into the
> past. Even what we have forgotten, what has escaped from our
> consciousness, is not erased from the world; it has become part of
> the past, and it remains part of the world.
> —Viktor E. Frankl, *The Unheard Cry for Meaning*

In March of 1991, my father died from Alzheimer's disease
while living in a nursing home in Stuart, Florida. In the summer of
1992, I began writing a book about him in an attempt to recover
what I thought had been irretrievably lost—his life. I was increas-
ingly and desperately frustrated when I tried to write about him
because I felt such an absence, not only of the present, but of
the past as well. During that same summer, Hurricane Andrew,
called the most destructive hurricane of the twentieth century, hit
the coast of Florida. I remember watching the news on television,
unbelievable scenes of houses flying down deserted streets, piers
ripping from pilings, cars leaning against vacant buildings. In
particular, I remember one scene of a family returning to their
oceanfront home to find it gone entirely: no foundation, no
framing, no wood, no nails. All that remained was the constant
pounding of the surf against an empty beach, and it occurred to me
that the devastation caused by Hurricane Andrew was analogous to
my family's experience with Alzheimer's disease. I realized that I felt
exactly the same way the family returning to their beach home felt:
completely and utterly shocked. It wasn't just my father's death that
was so devastating, but the perception that the disease, like the
hurricane, had washed everything away, swirling our lives into some
irretrievable black hole. Our collective memory, like the beach
house, seemed gone forever, erased completely.

1

Yet in *The Unheard Cry for Meaning* Viktor Frankl assures us that disease, death, or any violent action cannot obliterate our lives. He asserts that our lives, our pasts, each moment that trickles by, are safely deposited into a past that is protected from any calamity we may encounter. "Nothing and nobody can deprive and rob us of what we have safely delivered and deposited in the past. In the past, nothing is irretrievably and irrecoverably lost, but everything is permanently stored." If this is true, then my father's life and my life with him, while seeming to be gone (like the beach house), is actually *somewhere.*

I started to think more about the hurricane. When Andrew came screeching down the Florida coast, sweeping houses, cars, buildings, and everything else up into its terrible fury, while at first glance those things seemed to have "disappeared," they had actually been deposited *somewhere* else. For example, a car may be at the bottom of the ocean, or a beach house, now in pieces, may lie deep within the sand, but the point is that they still *exist* somewhere in some form, and are, therefore, retrievable. These objects do exist outside the experience of destruction, as Frankl asserts, and not only can we retrieve them, but we can also rebuild them if we choose. We could, with enough work and effort, gather all the pieces—grab a roof here, gather floor boards there, pull shingles from the shallows off the pier, dig deep enough in the sand to find the walls and support beams—and reassemble the house.

While retrieval might be difficult, it is possible. The house can actually be rebuilt. Yet, this house will not be the house it once was. Yes, each piece has been retrieved and reassembled, each nail found, each gutter replaced, but something has happened to the house—it has taken on new life. Particles from the ocean floor are now imbedded in the floor planks, shards of sea glass in the wainscoting; starfish cling to the clapboards on the raised back porch; the windowpanes are scratched from the sand; and tiny barnacles have made a home in the shingles on the back roof.

When I began this book, there was so much I didn't know about my father's life, and it took the perception of its eradication to force me to rebuild it through journals, interviews, conversations, letters, and creative imaginings. As I started to reassemble my father's life, a strange phenomenon started happening—I began to stumble across connecting links between my narrative and the world at large. I was literally led to books, articles, and pieces of information that seemed somehow connected to our family life, pieces that called me to include them. For example, while I was writing a story my father once told us about the prospects of being the missing link in the history of evolution, I came across an article about an ancient fish, the coelacanth, believed to have been extinct for millions of years yet discovered alive in the twentieth century. Somehow the presumed disappearance of the coelacanth and my father's tale about a missing link attached themselves, for me, to my father's actual disappearance as he slowly deteriorated from Alzheimer's disease.

The act of reassembly has allowed me to see that the portals of past experience often preview the future, and that along with the recollection of memory comes a myriad of other attachments. What I have found is that my father's life, like the beach house, has taken on new life. A new world has attached itself to the old, and it is teeming with new possibilities and directions.

While at times this "new life" has become complicated and confusing, seeming to replicate the experience of the disease, it has provided me with a comfort in knowing that every experience is buoyed by others and that we are never alone in our sorrow or in our joy. Even the Alzheimer's, which in this book actually has a voice and a personality of its own, is flanked by other moments and experiences that take some of the isolation and devastation away.

As a young man, my father wrote a letter to my mother, who was away on a trip. In the letter, he has put my sisters and me to bed and writes, ". . . after a riotous evening, the diapers are sloshing in the laundry, the bulbs are in, the storm window is back in place . . . we are all intact." Writing this manuscript has led me to believe that yes, indeed, we are all intact.

This book is a collage of my family's life, the life that brimmed and brims around us still.

Rim

He was the longest thing I ever saw,
as tall as a house,
about seven of me.

Our walks were amazing.
He'd tilt almost
over forward
                    slip
topple back,
hurl me through the air,
                    like a startled bird,
all without
a single word.

Then he'd hold me
                    crooked
look straight ahead

him smiling me smiling at him
                    the light
                            catching the rim.

Part One

Dream   *I am standing outside on a long, dark street looking at the moon. I've been told by a high-pitched voice in the trees that my father's disease can be arrested by the lack of gravity on the moon and that if we let him live there, he will not be sick anymore. I'm trying to bargain with the voice, asking for a deal of some kind. Could we visit him, a week maybe, anything? But it is an absolute deal and once he is on the moon, he's there forever. All I can do is look up at night and hope to see a small line walking across the tiny surface, maybe the blur of his hand waving.*

The Wing

I am aware that the man sitting on the porch looks like my father, the white shock of hair certainly the same, his torso too long, his legs like pencils with eraser feet. Kneeling beside him is the figure of my sister, arm plopped on his right knee. She is leaning into the scene as if to hear every word, giving the impression of something cozy and gathering. The checkered back of my other sister disappears around the side of the porch. My mother hovers behind the rocking chair, resting her hand on his hunched shoulder, patting, smoothing the wrinkled white T-shirt. She is looking off into the distance, at the hills perhaps, the dark, smooth humps that line the vista from the nursing home. I raise my hand to wave, but hold it there instead in a kind of promise-to-tell-the-truth-the-whole-truth-and-nothing-but-the-truth position. My mother looks over and for one skip of a moment I hope she won't know me, will keep scanning the parking lot for some other daughter to come sailing in to join the family that is about to leave this man behind.

The building looks like a huge face with ranks of window-mouths oouuing and ahhing. Lots of landscaped areas give the impression of careful planning to ensure a look of serenity and peace: gladiolas, stargazers, hollyhocks, and asiatic lilies wave a gentle invitation to the steady stream of traffic whizzing by. In the center of the building, a gigantic darkened doorway seems to suck the light out of the day and devour it. People struggle to open a faulty screen door that sticks and wiggles. Looking like odd circus performers doing tricks, they lean forward and back, forward and back, forward and into the black corridor inside, where they disappear like ghosts.

Working on the side of the building, a very suntanned man with a blue shirt tied around his head pushes a red wheelbarrow at high speed towards bags of topsoil and cedar mulch. He scoots the barrow and drops it, wraps a huge tangle of muscle around three bags at once, and thawumps them down. Then he grabs three more, hefts them even higher, flaps them on the stack, grabs the handles with open palms, and races to the half-moon shaped garden. In one push, the bags tumble onto the ground. One bag has ripped open, and dark, red chunks of bark spill onto the lawn like guts from a fish.

"Mom," I holler, dipping slightly in a rut in the path. "Hey." She nods, as does my sister, and I do some sort of skip hop jump onto the first step of the porch. Dad raises his head in slow motion.

"Dad," I say, giving him a hug-hug, pat-pat on the back.

My other sister appears on the porch, swinging through the shadows as if she were a hostess about to welcome guests. Strands of sweaty blond hair frame her face like tiny shutters. "His room is ready. The nurse took me down . . . we spruced things up a bit . . . put flowers. It's really very nice." She stands behind Dad and pats him on the shoulder. "Dad, why don't we . . ." Then to us in a whisper, "The nurse says they are going to call everyone in soon. Some men are coming to take down that dying elm tree over there," she points vaguely, "so we should . . . Dad?" she sings, kneeling beside my other sister, who is now watching a row of ants march across the gray porch floor. "Let's go inside." He nods, seeming to agree, then goes rigid and stiff, locking his knees together, rooting himself. Mom does kind of a burp-burp thing on his back as if that will blast him forward. One sister leans over and talks right at him as if that will help; the other sister keeps staring at the floor. I reach over and begin to gently prod an elbow loose, working it like a machinist lubing a stuck nut, then hoist him to his feet that seem glued to the floor. I touch the base of his calf, tap it the way one taps horses to clean their hooves. Eventually, he picks up a foot and plops it down, picks and plops, and we begin to move, the entire family, like a giant paramecium dividing and subdividing, towards the door.

Inside, no one says anything about the smells of urine and Clorox. "Oh, look, a piano, how lovely. Dad, see, you can play here. They must have gatherings." Shuffle shuffle we move and turn. "The paintings are nice. I like Jesus over the mantle, dear, isn't that nice?" More turning, sliding past food trays and stained bed sheets, heaps of towels and toiletries. A crunched old man in a metal wheelchair waves as we pass. A woman with a walker touches my sleeve and I flinch away.

As the corridor begins to narrow, the three of us, the children, fall back, and Mom loops her arm through Dad's in an after-you-are-married-walking-down-the-aisle-now-you're-mine kind of gesture. He turns his head towards her and she pats his forearm in reassurance, smiling as best she can. We follow silently until we're all standing before the cool steel door with the tiny window, the one through which we see lines of shuffling people moving in glazed circles. "Just push the button," one sister says, and she reaches up and presses the black disk with the thumb of her right hand.

piano

"play 'hark the herald angels sing'," my mother whispers
in his ear at christmas. he is sitting at a beautiful black
piano next to the window at the nursing home where my
grandmother lives. he is all shiny in a dark suit with fancy
buttons and a wild tie that looks like christmas in a blender.

he tips his head a bit as if he hears something way back in
his mind, then nods to some invisible person. his hands move
so quickly over the keys that it is easy to get a headache
trying to follow his fingertips; they just fly like birds let out of a
cage. and the things he can make with those hands, the most
amazing notes that hang on in the air even after they close the
top of the piano and wheel everyone into the hall.

"ready girls?" my mother says from behind my dad. we, my
two sisters and i, are standing over next to a sort-of-tree-
sort-of-bush that leans forward like it is listening or learning
something new. "ready?" she says, as she plops herself
on the window behind him and plants her hand with all the
diamonds on his shoulder. i look at all the old people circled
around us like a fire. i love-hate doing this every year. it
always makes me cry to watch these guys clap for us like
we are the mormon tabernacle choir, which we aren't even
close to. they would clap even if we all were a bunch of
wolves howling. they just like us being here, paying so much
attention to them since they never get any.

when he plays the music for the old people, he seems even
taller, like maybe eight feet of just sheer happiness and joy.

his fingers pound the keys and lift way up as if he is giving
the audience and me and my sisters a huge wave, and then
his hand lands back down on exactly the right keys. he puckers
up his mouth looking all lemon-swallowed, and throws his head
around, happy because by now he practically is the piano.

when we need a break from the christmas stuff, he makes
up songs, that's how good he is. he makes up songs
with instructions in them for us kids to do something or
else sometimes even for him or my mother to do something.
his favorite is "daddy's got to spray the roses now, pretty
roses, daddy's got to spray the roses now, but mama bear,
mama bear, mama bear better get out there, and put away the
lawnmower right now." then my mother will chime in, "never,
never, never, never, never right now!" all of us know that dad
isn't really asking my mother to put away the lawnmower
since she doesn't do the outside chores. and she knows
it, too, but will make this big face when she sings the song
like "how dare he ask me to move a dirty machine into the
garage." my mother can be very dramatic with her hands all
whooshing in the air, gold rings clicking together. she makes
my dad smile and throw his head back—this is the life for him.

Howard

"'O Lord, God of my salvation, I have cried day and night before thee; O let my prayer enter into thy presence, incline thine ear unto my calling. . . .'" Howard (we don't know his last name) is reading from his wrinkled bed to my father from a Book of Psalms he keeps on the nightstand. Dad is sitting in his rocking chair looking all scrunched, seeming to make himself smaller, more compact, as if he's a circus act preparing to shoot out of a cannon and into a safety net, if only it were that easy to find safety now.

Howard is my father's roommate, and in his former life, before he became an Alzheimer's patient, he was an Episcopalian minister, which he still is really because that's what he does all day, reads from the Bible or from his Book of Psalms. Often he reads in the hallway, walking back and forth like a member of a choir, nodding at whatever he is passing by, pretending, perhaps, that he is addressing his flock, helping them through the difficulties of their lives, though he is beyond that himself at this point, no help in sight, the disease hovering over him like a giant wave.

"'For my soul is full of trouble; and my life draweth nigh unto the grave.'"

"Treble mum," Dad mutters, fidgeting with the air as if trying to rearrange its molecular structure.

"It's okay, Dad, just sit back. Why don't you close your eyes?" I say, smoothing his sweater and pulling his collar out from the neck. His skin is dry and almost translucent in places, as if I could look right through and into him.

"'I am counted as one of them that go down into the pit, and I am even as a man that hath no strength.'"

Howard is much smaller than my father and quite round, like a little ball of cookie dough. He is completely bald and has a nervous habit of running his right hand back and forth over the top of his head, polishing it. By the end of the day he looks like a shiny missile as he paces and reads. With his head down, one might think Howard were a bullet heading for its mark.

"'Thou hast laid me in the lowest pit, in a place of darkness, and in the deep.'"

"Howard, how are you doing today?" my mother asks as she sits down next to him. He looks up from his book.

"I'm fine today. And breakfast was delicious, which he didn't eat you know," he says, pointing a finger at my eyes-closed father.

"Well, I'm glad you ate it. You need to keep up your strength," she smiles, patting him on the leg.

"And I do. I eat everything they give me. No questions."

It seems that Howard rarely gets any visitors, maybe just a distant daughter, who comes every other week or so with a huge box of candy and some silly child's toy like a pinwheel or bubbles. She rarely stays more than thirty minutes, usually sitting in Dad's chair staring at Howard, not talking to him, not touching him, just watching as if he were a TV program that gets turned off. After half an hour, she stands up, gives him a peck on the cheek, and races down the hall to the locked steel door, which she bangs on way too hard, to get out.

"'Thou has put away mine acquaintance far from me. . . . I am so fast in prison that I cannot get forth.'"

"Howard, did you know that we are Episcopalian also? Bob taught Sunday school?"

"I didn't know that. He didn't say anything." Howard closes his Book of Psalms, keeping a thumb in his place.

"Yes, at St. Luke's. Where we lived when the girls were growing up. He studied quite hard."

"Bob?" he asks, looking towards Dad, who slowly lowers his head until it is level with his chest.

"Who?" Dad asks, looking as if he might cry.

"Remember, dear, how you taught Sunday school? I was telling Howard . . ."

"Fiddly school?" he asks again.

"Yes, that's right, dear. Howard, how about a chocolate?" Mom reaches for the huge box from last week's visit and offers one to Howard, who takes four. Then he looks back down to his book and his thumb-remembered place.

"'Shall thy wondrous works be known in the dark? and thy righteousness in the land where all are forgotten?'"

Dream   *In the dream, I walk into his room and find him covered in blue feathers, a huge birdman oozing blood and goo, leaking kidney and liver and heart and lungs and brain into a stain on the floor. I grab armloads of white gauze as if I were some strange wedding attendant. I am trying to shove at him, push-mop-jam it back, but it is coming, gushing—the overflow—and he is smaller, just a boy, jerking curling deep under, and he's a baby, he's erasing, he's my "father, son and holy . . . now and forever," he is born, he is dying, coming and going, he is a shadow, "and the life of the world to come, amen."*

Man-Child

"We can't let Mom take him home," my sister says over the phone line that cracks and spits into the late evening. "She can't handle it. He's gone beyond."

"What happened?" I ask.

"Mom and Dad, you know, came for the weekend. A visit. He was okay, or so it seemed. Quiet. Like he's been. Just sitting there." I imagine my father, the man-child, propped up in a blue chaise, looking ready for a photograph at some occasion. And everyone in the room trying to look at each other, not at him, have a conversation about something else, like the news or a neighbor.

"He chased the boys around the house," she says. "Put his shirt on backwards, took his pants off. The label sticking out looked like another tongue. They thought he was a monster."

My father has a very particular way of walking now. He sort of clumps along, picking one foot up higher than the other. Clump foot, blump foot, that's how he looks. And his ankles crack so loudly it sounds like he is breaking apart. The last time I visited, I remember being curled in bed listening to Mom help him up the stairs. I could hear the cracking getting louder and slower with each step, and I remember holding my breath wondering if he would make it to bed without dying in the process.

"I can't imagine," I say, picturing him with his hair all raised the way it gets now, looking like broken wheat. I can see his skinny legs moving like a chicken flap-flapping around my sister's kitchen.

"And he gets so angry," she says. "Yells and screams. Told us all he's in charge, and we better do what he says. The way he shook his fist," she sinks down a note, "scared me to death."

"If she can't take him home, what are we going to do with him?" I ask. "He can't stay with you guys. She's got to go back. . . ." My sister tells me about the procedure of getting him into a nursing home. First, he will go to the hospital, driven by the police because he is a danger to himself and others. Then, after three days, he will be released to a place that can take him.

I remember the day I first saw the change. I was visiting for Christmas, when we always tried to make each moment a Kodak one so that we could all come away feeling successful. Pictures would help, lots of them with us all smiling the famous Smith grin no matter what's going on inside. My mother and I were in the kitchen cleaning up breakfast. Dad had disappeared upstairs, probably to take a shower and get dressed. Then all of a sudden he appeared in the doorway with his blue hooded bathrobe on, looking like a grim reaper. He had a wastebasket in his hand, holding it up near his head, as if measuring it. Or maybe he was listening to it. Or maybe he was going to put it on his head like a hat.

I waited for him to say something, but he just stayed there against the counter looking totally exhausted, as if he might collapse. It was then that I realized his mind was outside himself now, the way your shadow lays out when the sun is behind and you try to catch it, step on yourself, but when you do, you only step on darkness. I knew that for the life of him he didn't know what to do with the wastebasket. And I don't mean should he empty it in here or out in the garage—I mean that he didn't know what a wastebasket was for. And from that moment on, I never saw my real father again.

"I'll call you later," I tell my sister, and hang up the phone. Outside, the streetlight flashes huge patches on the lawn, and I wonder what it must be like for him now, living with this terrible referee running around inside his brain calling for a time out.

Moondaze

1.

The burden comes in pieces:
a sea-green velvet promise
blue iguana—
  a rising throat.

2.

In the summer huge zucchini
fill the garden,
wrapped in madness
  rimmed in gold.

3.

Treeline bushes yellow:
bird-checks hover,
glitterflipping quarters
  bought and sold.

4.

Isn't this extinction?
a species-cloaking
solo darkness—
  a final note.

Looking for Warm

The temperature of my father's childhood was about 60 degrees. "Because it's good for your digestion," his parents said. He'd go to bed right after dinner just to be warm. When he walked, he would clench his fists, then open and close them repeatedly, as if trying to generate more heat and hold it, like a little built-in furnace.

He was born in Canada, which didn't help the cold thing. I'll bet they had to swaddle him in a zillion blankets, not just one, after the birth. He probably came out and before he breathed hello to the world took a look at the thermostat and asked the nurse to turn it up. He was just a big Popsicle inside, an ice cube that never melted.

And all that snow in Canada. As the only boy, he was always stuck shoveling, which he hated, of course, because it was so cold. Back then, there were no heated boots and socks, no little packets of heat to put in gloves and shirt pockets. So he'd shovel and shiver and maybe once in a while some hot cocoa would come his way, but then he'd look at the sky, more snow, and he'd be back at it. His sisters probably felt sorry for him, maybe knit him a hat or passed extra food his way to help put some fat on his bones, which he needed, being just a skinny little thing. His mother probably looked at him at the dinner table, after he ate the biggest meal, and said something about keeping his strength up, with a pat to his leg maybe under the table so his dad wouldn't see.

So you'd think after all this he'd move to the Caribbean or something when he got a chance, say see ya snow and hop a plane south, which he did, come south, but only to the United States, becoming a citizen with the right to shovel snow in America now, which he did, because he stopped too soon and landed in New York. Not that the weather there was as bad as in Canada, but it was cold, and he had to buy overcoats and galoshes and wool stuff, and he spent the next 30 years of his life in a constant shiver, blowing into his cupped hands as if trying to hold his breath for later.

And that just continued when he got a family, the freezing-to-death part. He was always turning up the heat, not just a little, but turning that dial up around 80, so he could stop shaking and having to wear two sweaters. Of course, the rest of us would have to go upstairs and open our windows, stand in front of them, take deep breaths to try and erase that heat smell that seemed to permeate the air. Sometimes we'd have to shake ourselves awake, feeling on the verge of a death sleep. Friends used to joke that when they came over they'd have to wear bathing suits and flip-flops as if it were perpetual summer at our house.

Mom used to say that she was sure he would have been a happier man if he'd only been brought up in the South. Maybe none of this would have happened.

So it's really not surprising that one day when he was 55 he just decided that enough was enough, he'd had it. He told Mom that he wanted to move south, packed a suitcase and a thermos of Quik, hopped into his TR-6, and said, "I'll call you when I find our new home." Then off he sped in search of a thermometer that constantly read 70 or above. Of course, we all knew he was headed to Florida, because the weather maps on TV always show it with a smiling sun over the whole state, so where else would he go.

After about a week, he called and told Mom he'd found it. Stuart, Florida, right on the Intercoastal Waterway, would be their next home. His voice was smiling when he talked about the water and palm trees, how the breezes made him feel big and strong, how the days were long and sunny. He got a real estate agent to begin looking for a home, then came back to begin packing.

Mom wasn't too thrilled about moving since she loved her home and wasn't the one shivering, but Dad was persistent, so she went along with it, which is often what a wife does.

So off they zoomed one Saturday afternoon, Mom in the station wagon and Dad in his glory, shifting gears faster than ever before on his little car, blazing onto the highway like a fire.

Conversation: I

Joan: I don't remember him sick. I didn't see him from that July until he died

Polly: Yeah, you were lucky. But remember that trip

Joan: When the illness was showing itself. Don't you remember that, Mom, that nightmare trip to Canada? It was bad. It was the next year

Mom: I remember we had just come through Vermont, on our way to the Thousand Islands. We stopped at a gas station. Dad wanted to put gas in the car. In the Buick Skylark. He took the leaded nozzle

Joan: And I told him take the other one. And he turned on me. It was not Dad standing there. He called me a little bitch. He brooded in the back. I grabbed his hand and said, Dad, I don't want to fight, I am really sorry

Mom: When I got back in the car

Joan: He said, I don't need you to look after me. Fine, I told him, from now on I am not going to continue to take care of you, and I just floored it out of there. And you, mother, were so upset about it. And he was so ungracious later about my apology. He was still clinging to the thought that he could take care of things. And that was devastating to him. For this little whipper-snapper to presume that she knew more about cars than he did

Mom: When we got to Canada, it was really hard and we decided to leave two days early. It was horrible, watching it happen all over again. Just like his sister Marion

Joan: I felt so bad. How could I say something like that? How could I be so mean

Cathy: Because you are human. You are not a saint

Mom: It wasn't Dad talking, saying those awful things. He was possessed. It was the voice of the Alzheimer's speaking. When he lashed out, it was the Alzheimer's. When he said *period,* that was the end of conversation. I don't remember ever voicing an opinion. We never had cross words until then. You two went to Canada the summer before—he was difficult then, too

Cathy: We kept setting alarms to make sure that he took the medication. Sitting around the table talking about Aunt Marion. He kept looking for her, like her ghost might waft through the room. And he started talking about the time in Batavia, New York, when a cop stopped him. He went on and on about it, and he was so angry, and he was pounding the table as if he could never forget it, never, even after he died

Mom: Dad had rage. Where did that come from? Not knowing how to direct your anger. I don't remember Daddy really getting angry in front of anyone. We didn't argue. My parents didn't argue. I think Daddy had a lot of rage because he wasn't really where he wanted to be. He should have been a teacher, an artist, a sailing instructor—those lovely, much gentler pursuits. But his father insisted he pursue some kind of profession. So he became a lawyer because you did what your dad said

Polly: I think he lived with Thoreau in that quiet desperation

Cathy: Dad had that great vegetable garden in the backyard of our house at 29 Briar Brae, and he would check for beans

Joan: I couldn't even tell you about the back of the house. Where was the door

Polly: You could go in the front door

Cathy: I would remember Dad dragging clippings behind the little piece of fence. He always seemed to be appearing from behind something, happy as a clam. He would pull up the burlap tarp with a big hole in it and a couple of leaves scampering behind him

Joan: I can remember him down in the living room probably the best. I don't remember him in the kitchen

Mom: Yes, we had the breakfast table and the door outside and the door of the little family room

Cathy: And I can remember him taking us saucering down the front hill and across the street and off we'd go woosh. And he planted daffodils

Polly: I remember Dad more at our other house, at 23 Briar Brae. With the community center. All that outside work he would do. He never wanted to be alone, but he always was. I remember just sitting out there with him while he put in a bunch of bricks on the wall. I think he put a picture of us in there

Cathy: Remember the snake in the dryer

Mom: Oh, God, yes, he reached in for pants or something and there it was. It was huge, six feet long. Came up the dryer vent

Cathy: He must have screamed bloody murder. And then how he filled all the snake holes in the yard with cement. He was always battling with nature, trying to keep it outside where it belonged

Joan: He was always painting a room or putting up wallpaper, and he used to love to sit on the front porch and watch the thunderstorms come over the city

Mom: He loved Florida when we moved there. He loved the sky

Polly: Dad always seemed to be home. If you knew where to look for him, you could find him

Joan: You would come in the door and he would be sitting at the counter and I would hop up on the counter and just sit there and talk with him forever. "Oh, let's have a glass of Quik," he would say, and I'd start reaching into the cupboard

Polly: He always sat in central places so that he wouldn't be passed by. He wanted to be right in the thick of things. He would sit in those black chairs that swirled, or you could find him on the porch. I can remember him painting the floor

Joan: That long chain he wore would whack him in the head every time he leaned over. One time all his cigarettes fell into a can of paint

Mom: He loved hardware stores. Right near the bank, near the intersection. Do you remember the bank where we said good-bye? The hardware store had a section with teacups and Dad would fiddle and piddle forever

Joan: It wasn't too far from the fire station. There was a little hardware store near the delicatessen. Mr. Winters owned it. When he sold out, the Happy Spirit Shop opened up, which is where Dad spent so much of his time

Polly: That flight of stairs went straight up, that was the back door to the liquor store. How many people slipped in and slipped out of that place with their bottles? It was a big drop

Nonstop Service to West Palm

"Ladies and gentlemen, on behalf of US Airways and this Atlanta-based crew, I'd like to welcome you aboard US Airways flight 1694 nonstop service to West Palm Beach. If you would take a moment to locate the instruction sheet placed in the seat jacket in front of you . . ."

I reach for the card but instead slide out the airsick bag clipped over the *US Airways Sky Mall* magazine, wondering how much puke the thing can really hold. I take off my sunglasses, turn my neck from side to side.

"Simply insert the buckle and pull the strap tight. To release, simply pull the buckle up. . . ."

The plane is pretty full, which I hate because it means the more luggage, the more weight, and the quicker the crash. I believe the lighter we are, the better our chances are of staying up in the sky.

The woman sitting next to me hasn't moved since I sat down. I look over and see she has something on her lap that looks like a rock. She sees me staring and pulls her legs closer together. The rock thing tips a bit, and a little head pokes out.

"Is that real?" I whisper, bending towards her as if this should be our secret.

"Oh, yes. His name is Ben," she responds, holding it closer so I can inspect. "He's a box turtle."

Ben pulls his head all the way in as she holds him closer. His shell looks like a tapestry of hopscotch. "Do you take him with you like this all the time?"

"Always. It's legal, you know."

"Oh." I tap the top of his shell lightly. "Hi, Ben."

I jump as a stewardess leans over us. "You are both seated in an emergency exit row. In case of a situation, you would be required to open the hatch by turning the wheel and pulling it towards you. It weighs about 50 pounds. Do you feel comfortable with this?" I nod, sliding the puke bag back into the seat jacket. Of course I'm comfortable with that, I'm sitting here for just that reason. I want to be the first one out.

The turtle lady asks to be reseated, stuffing Ben into her purse and jumping up. I unbuckle myself and plunk out into the aisle to let her pass by. "Have a good trip," I say to her as she slides by me. I picture Ben nose down like a tube of lipstick.

It's as I sit down again that I notice him, his blond cloud curls sticking up like little gnomes. He is two rows ahead of me on the right, in the aisle seat, sitting perfectly still as if screwed in. His shoulders have that sway that means he is tired, has been working too long in the garden. I am so sure it's my father that I actually start wondering what he is doing here, why he isn't getting ready to come to the airport with Mom, waiting for me to glide out of the gateway with my big smile so they can both smile back, and we can all smile and smile and how-was-your-trip each other to death. How has he managed to get on the plane?

"From the flight deck, this is Captain Harris. We are waiting for a few more pieces of luggage to be loaded and we'll be underway. . . ."

I turn to look out the window to see if I recognize the last-minute baggage the two blue-uniformed and headphoned young men are throwing onto the conveyer belt, to see if I can zero in on the gold RDS insignia Mom had engraved for his birthday one year. But only a dilapidated cardboard box, a green backpack, and a bag of golf clubs disappear into the plane below.

More people slide by in the aisle, all red-faced and thank-god-I-made-it looking, flipping open overhead compartments looking for space. One guy starts huffing to the stewardess that everything is full and where can he put his briefcase. She gives him a how-about-being-on-time-buster look, then smiles and offers to store the case up front.

Maybe Dad has split himself into two people, like Superman did on that episode when he had to be Clark Kent and Superman at the same time, how he summoned up all his strength and shook himself in half. Then the new guy stepped away from the old guy and they looked exactly alike and the assumption was they were both okay. But as the show went on, each one became weak and frail, stumbling on sidewalks, holding on to lampposts for balance. Maybe that's what's wrong with Dad; somehow he split in half.

The plane bumpthumps once and we are on our way. Dad just sits there, doesn't look out the window, scratch his head, cough. Just sits.

"This is Captain Harris from the flight deck. We are number one for departure. Flight attendants, please prepare the cabin for takeoff."

I lean towards the window seat that is empty without the turtle lady. The plane does the big roar thing, pauses, then begins to speed down the runway, 30, 35, 40 seconds, 41, then slowly raises its nose into the air. Pieces of tree and sky merge as we draw a line between heaven and earth.

You could come back and sit with me, Dad. Take the extra seat. Stretch out your legs.

I look ahead at him, picture his chiseled, sunburned nose that gets purple without sunscreen and looks like he still drinks too much. The tooth with the gold chip. Taut lips and funny, maybe-we-could-tie-them-down ears.

Come here.

". . . When we reach a cruising altitude, the flight attendants will come around. . . ."

Eventually the stewardess pushes through with a too-full cart of bottles of drink. I see her lean over Dad to speak to the head two seats away, nod, then speak to the one in the next seat, nodding again. She skips over Dad and goes for a couple of minibottles of clear alcohol. Probably vodka. A ten-dollar bill appears to come out of the top of Dad's head. She nods again, passes back two ones. Then she leans in so close to Dad I'm sure she will kiss him. Her eyebrows rise, she shakes her head, raises her eyebrows again, nods, and pushes the cart away.

He still hasn't moved. He must be asleep. Or dead.

For the rest of the trip I hold my *New Yorker* magazine open on my lap, play with the latch on the tray that I didn't use to drink my apple juice, watch the seat-belt sign to make sure it stays off. Eventually, I begin to thumb through the *US Airways Magazine* and begin reading an article about coelacanths: large, blue-gray, very ugly fish that were believed to be extinct.

"This is Captain Harris from the flight deck. We are about 60 miles east of West Palm Beach and have begun our descent. Flight crew, please prepare the cabin for landing."

By fish standards, the coelacanth is a giant, measuring almost five feet in length, all speckled, with fins that look more like legs. Sort of like a dog or something. But the really amazing thing about the coelacanth is that a living one was found.

I look up and rub my eyes. I can feel the plane beginning to nose down and remember that the landing is the most dangerous part of the trip. I look back down to the article.

". . . We ask that you return your tray table and seat to their upright positions. . . ."

I flip the rest of the pages quickly, skim a new diet that uses bark from trees, and slide the magazine back into the seat jacket. Since I never look out the window when landing, I just watch Dad in the seat ahead, wondering when the heck he will get up and notice me. Maybe he's mad, angry that I only visit occasionally. Maybe he knows what's up.

Suddenly, he turns his head to the right, revealing a slim, ski-jump nose and . . . it's not him. It's some younger guy with old hair. He stands, opens the overhead compartment, and pulls out a green computer bag and a brown sweater, which he flips around his neck and ties into place.

We land with a thump, up thump down, put-your-hand-on-the-seat-in-front-of-you-until-we-slow (and-don't-skid-off-the-end-into-the-water) kind of experience. The plane cuts across the runway and speeds towards the terminal. This is actually my favorite part of the trip, driving around in this big thing. Sometimes I think this would be the best way to take a plane trip—just drive it down the highway, watching movies and eating snacks. No air involved.

"On behalf of US Airways and this Atlanta-based crew, I'd like to welcome you to West Palm Beach. The local time is 12:30 P.M. . . ."

Unbuckling my seatbelt, I decide to slide into the aisle quickly, even though I am jumping the line. Crooked people hovering just under the call buttons and reading lights glare at me, so I look up as if fascinated with the hanging projection screen.

The captain and first mate shake-shake-thank-you as we leave the plane, hoping we'll all come back and see them again sometime, make the exciting and life-changing decision to choose US Airways over another carrier. I nod and heft my bag onto my shoulder; the weight bumps against my back as my stiff, tired legs amble up the metal ramp and onto the carpeted gateway that will lead me out into the waiting area where one-and-a-half parents are waiting.

Disease-Man

When I get sick, real sick,
and my brain lies open and I
begin to go insane, I can visit the
animals at the zoo all day, watch
them lumber about their cages
lurching back and forth, their
wildness sliding off like molted
skin. Maybe I could get a job
there, a huge man with an empty
brain, taking the trash out and
sweeping up the silence. Or else
I could take care of the dead ones,
bury them in the choked forest
where all abandoned animals
return home.

Linger

to the upbeat flight of memories
the flagged beats of the running heart
—Alice Walker

Before I know it, I'm a mile
out of town. No traffic or
loud voices, just the splash of water
along the rocks. I forget
how dark dark is, catch myself
tripping on stones, lurching,
losing track. A group of ducks
keep up, quack back,
reminding me, perhaps,
to keep straight,
    follow the path.

Out of the field looms
a powerline, giant robot
like something landed.
I stand beneath it,
look up, see a woman
dance in the sky,
her belly booming in and out
as the clouds hurry, a thick
whirl of passion, then
nothing,
    only stars.

The far grass moves as if
someone is passing. I imagine
an alien encounter, a whisking
away to another planet, hear only
the crack of static overhead,
a fist tapping a Morse code
into the giant ear
  of night.

People vanish like that,
quickly, a last moment of light,
incredible color,
an eerie presence, a linger
of smoke. A moment.
Like pulling sound
through a tunnel, a
thin piercing
  of skin.

Baggage

Judy and Bob Smith are standing as far away from the gate as is possible to stand yet still be counted as meeting-your-party. Dad's striped Izod shirt makes him look like an oversized candy cane; Mom has on a bright pink, shifty thing that seems cool and peppermint-ice-creamish. "Hello, dear," she says, floating towards me and kissing me on the cheek.

"Hi, Mom. Hi, Dad," I say, patting his shoulder like he needs calming down. He smiles wanly; he is even thinner than last time, as if he is a piece of taffy people are pulling and pulling until it breaks in the center so they can pile it into their mouths and swallow.

"Is this it?" Mom asks, pointing to my shoulder bag.

"No, one suitcase. I'll get it if you guys want to sit down."

"We're fine, dear," she says, and we begin to move towards the other end of the terminal. Dad towers over us both, his chin almost right-angled ahead as if following a plumb line. His hands hang limply at his sides, and I think about holding one but don't.

My suitcase pops out through the plastic curtain that looks as if someone cut it into strips by accident. I reach and grasp the handle, setting the suitcase down at my feet. Dad leans over and grabs the handle with his right hand; he tries to lift it but can't.

"That's okay, Dad, I've got it." He moves closer to the bag, sits down on the edge of the conveyer belt, and sighs.

"Dad, I've got it."

"What is this?" he asks.

"What, that?" I point to the suitcase.

"What is it?" he asks again. "What's it for?"

"My clothes. So I can visit."

"So you can visit," he nods.

"Come on, Dad, let's go," I say, and gently put a finger on the bone of his arm. He jerks away angrily, then stares ahead without looking at either of us. I look at my mother. She shakes her head.

"Dad, we've got to go. Come on. . . ."

He won't budge, and it's a problem because crowds of people are trying to get their luggage. They have to reach around him, and they all look exasperated and huffy, and I'm thinking, please God, get him up. I realize I am trying to pretend that he's not really with me, that I am separate, off on my own, meeting my party outside—and I hate myself for it.

We wait for a half hour, long enough to see the red light blink its warning several times, more luggage coming, more luggage coming. Mom buys a Coke and stands in the corner with her arms crossed over her chest, pretending to read the instructions for tracking down lost baggage.

Then, suddenly, Dad gets up and starts for the revolving door. I grab my suitcase, yell "Mom," and we're off.

The ride to Stuart is quiet and hot. I drive, Dad sits in front, and Mom is in the back doing something with a pattern and yarn. Dad's playing a weird game with himself, itsy-bitsy-spidering his fingers along the tops of his knees as if he's playing an invisible piano. I glance up at the rearview mirror, but Mom is glued elsewhere.

We turn onto a side street by the water. Dad points out the window. "That's where she used to be," he says, and I know he means the little motorboat he just sold, the one he bought to remind his heart of the sea.

When he moved to Florida, my father wanted to get another boat. His sailing days were over—he was too old, my mother was no longer interested—so he resigned himself to buying a small, cute-as-a-powerboat-could-be craft that could maneuver in and out of the narrow waterways near his house. He said he only felt like half a skipper driving that thing because a real skipper wouldn't even consider it; a sailboat was the only vessel of a true captain.

Still, he enjoyed the elements in his surroundings, the gentle lap of the water against the hull when he anchored for lunch, the wind in his face as he paced the Intercoastal Waterway.

When it came time to name this boat—always an anxious situation because how exactly do you name a thing that is really supposed be a woman and so unpredictable—he knew that the name must have something to do with his wife, as everything in his life did. He decided on *Sandpiper,* which I initially thought was a ridiculous name compared to the names of our previous sailboats, names like *Blithe Spirit* and *Jezebel* that seemed to have a person singing behind them, names that when other boats passed our stern would attract attention, make people really think about us on the boat and our date with destiny, names that had violins playing in the background. Yet my father insisted that *Sandpiper* was the right name, after the birds that run along the beach chasing the waves in and out, those little poofs of energy that scud over the sand as if death were right behind them. He said that's how my mother ran, and he said it with such affection and such dramatic pause that the moment rang out and silenced everything around us, and I knew *Sandpiper* was it.

Remembering all this, I pull over and stop the car. "That," Dad says, pointing at a trawler, "is a Grand Banks. Beautiful boat." He opens the car door, gets out, and stands in the wind, watching. He seems happy for this moment, his blond curls dancing and glowing. Mom puts her knitting down and just watches him.

"Someone should be with him," she sighs, so I hop out and stand by his side.

"Isn't that the kind of boat you and Mom took that trip on?" I ask.

"It is indeed."

I think about staying here with him, maybe sitting for a while on the stone wall by the water, squinting into the wonderful sun. Or maybe even standing together, looking at our reflections in the water, how we would swerve and curve into gumpy figures. Maybe, in a quick flash of impulse, we could dive in, the two of us holding hands, into water where the leaving that is happening to him might cease in the weightless green haze, nothing to add or subtract, nothing more to happen in the peace of the sea.

I gaze at a sailboat struggling to come about, watch a family swing and dance across the deck of a white schooner, watch and watch, begging to see our family this time—sailor-man Dad standing over the tiller, steering with his foot; Mom curling up line and thawamping it in on the deck; me ready to hoist up the main; Polly and Joan lying on the top of the cabin in the sun.

Because if that were us, then I wouldn't have to pull into the driveway, put on the emergency brake. I wouldn't have to help him out of the car and look the other way when he stumbles. There would be no boxes in every room, no half-packed suitcases, no strange green stickers on the piano and melodeon. No brown wrapping tape around the lampshade, no paper plates with half-eaten pieces of pizza and potato salad. No empty bookcases, missing clocks, picture spaces, bare walls, open cupboards, chandelier in pieces. There would be no new condominium down the road to move into because Dad can't take care of the house anymore, no garden untended, no tag sale on Saturday, no one-car garage and where-will-we-put-the-other-car. There would be no new steps to navigate, no long hallway, no dark rooms, no new neighbors peeking, no street change, new address to memorize, vacant stare, no crying and pleading, no need to throw him a life preserver every two seconds.

No anguish, no grief, no praying to God for relief.

boat

he says, "come with me for the day, kitty-cat," and my mother makes up a cooler of sandwiches and chocolate milk and off we go to the boat.

when we get there, he jumps right in and starts pulling on the cord to get the motor to work. he pulls and pulls, hunching over the little question mark of a motor like he might just "boot it out into the water with one fell swoop," he says, jerking this way and that, and i watch the little flaps of skin on his back do jellodances. eventually the motor roars to life and he comes back to earth and sits right in front of me in this little boat that some guy gave us and called a skiff. it is a beat-up old thing with paint peeling like the skin on dad's back when it gets too much sun. anyway, here we are on the sound, dad's favorite place.

i'm feeling kind of hot and needing a drink of something, so i reach underneath the seat for the cold white box under there. i get this nip on my finger like what a puppy does when it first meets you. so i take a scream out of my lungs and throw it all around the boat, jumping up and down, which is exactly what daddy says never to do in a boat, especially a little one: "no lunatics allowed on the water." he turns the handle on the motor off really fast to suck the sound right out of the motor and out of me, too. all of a sudden it is really quiet except for the little kicking sound of the waves on the bottom of the boat. he asks me, "just what are you doing—don't you know never to stand up in a boat?" then he starts yelling and suddenly he jumps straight up in the air like the motor had

zoomed him up, too. there we are, both flapping around
in the wind like we're not supposed to do, arms and legs
kicking up at the sun and sky. i look down at his feet and see
all these little crabs that seem to be coming out of the water
and into the bottom of the boat, though i didn't know crabs
were like ghosts, just appearing out of nowhere.

then suddenly he just starts to laugh, that huge laugh that
begins way down the back of his neck when he throws his
head back like he is trying to hook the laugh and bring it
forward. i start laughing, too, just to be part of this occasion,
and at the same time, about a zillion of these tiny crabs
keep coming in through the bottom of the boat like they are
heading for home. daddy reaches down and picks up a huge
scoop of them with his big hands and flips them into this pail
he always brings in case we start sinking. he is quick about
it so none of them bite his fingers with those claws that look
like a too-big pair of scissors. then he says probably what is
happening is at night when the boat is lined up with the dock,
the crabs come right in and hide in the floorboards. when
we get in, he says, they are probably still sleeping and we
can't see them because they are all tucked in there out of
sight, but once we get going and things start to heat up,
they slither out looking to escape.

Gun

When I walk into the room, the nurses are changing his diaper. It is huge and wet, sagging to his knees, looking to be off and on at the same time. There is a nurse on each side coaxing him to sit. "So we can help you," one says. He opens his mouth to speak but just clicks his teeth like a shutter at low speed, click, click, click, as if trying to take a picture of another scene to insert into this one. After a minute he breaks away from their grip, shushing towards the bathroom in tiny fake steps, like a windup toy.

There is a moment when I think to run. Just back out. Pretend this is the wrong room and do an Etch-a-Sketch shake shake on the whole thing. Retreat into the hall, take a left, catch the elevator, press G, and wait for the safety of the closing door. Then walk nonchalantly past the stupid mural with the billy goats, place my hand on the metal push bar, and fling the door open into the hideous summer sun. Then just a few more steps to my mother's car, key in the lock, door open, gush into the leather seat, key in the ignition, and turn it on in an effort to pretend it was never off, has been running the whole time. Turn back out onto the highway and erase the memory of ever having taken the right turn in the first place, of ever having to take it again.

"You might want to wait in the lounge," the bigger nurse says to me, nodding in the direction of a few chairs and tables assembled at the end of the hall. "I'll come get you." At first I think, thank you, yes, I'll wait a billion years if you can just change him back into my father, yes, I'll just wait down there while you wave some magic wand or clunk him on the head if you have to, just get him out of those diapers and into a nice Sunday suit and we'll go to church or to Cobbs Mills for lunch, have a whisky sour and rum punch, eat all the cashews out of the nut mix, take two popovers instead of one, play with the electric windows in the Buick.

"It would be best," she says more emphatically, trying to hold my father from tipping over, tripping on the diaper that has now fallen to his ankles can you believe it? For God's sake, someone give him some underwear, cover him up, don't just leave him standing there, someone do something! Jesus.

"Dad . . . ," I say, my hands open as if holding some tangible thing to give him. "I'll be . . . right back."

"Please," he pleads. "Please." The nurses pick one leg up, then the other, and he wobbles like a sick penguin, one leg up, the other, and he tilts to the left, one leg, and he trips, then the other, and he pulls, one and the other, and they heave and he moves, and they drag him too hard and he pulls and they pull him to the bathroom through the door frame and inside.

I don't go far, just out into the hallway, pretending to examine the wallpaper, tracing the origin of each pink and green line and their exact points of intersection, as if calculating this mathematically could help to explain the complete disintegration of a brain. How is memory lost? Is it a slow trickling away, like sand pouring through an egg timer, three-minute intervals of loss, or does it fall out in chunks, handfuls of a person's life dropping away and rotting? And this: once lost, can memories ever live again in a healthy brain? Is there a halfway house somewhere in the universe that places these memories with new owners? Could a baby born in Oregon enter the world with a memory of skyscrapers and tankers along the Hudson River, mothers in fancy white cars, little girls in blue tutus swirling and twirling, and the cut and start of waves breaking over shores on Long Island Sound?

"There, now . . . let's just sit here, Mr. Smith." There is movement back in the room, so I poke my head in. Dad is dressed in blue slacks and a blue button-down shirt that needs to be ironed. He is shushing slowly towards his rocking chair, the chair my sister Polly bought him when he entered the first nursing home, in

North Carolina, the chair that was jammed in the car when he and Mom drove the ten hours back to Florida so she could bring him to this new place and go on with her life, the chair that will no doubt follow him into the next place, the one Mom and I are going to visit this afternoon, because "he can't stay here, we can't take care of him," the nurse said. "We don't have the facilities."

"Dad," I say gently and sit on the edge of the bed. I take his pale, mottled hand in mine, touch the ridges of raised blue veins— "blue blood means royalty," he used to say—that feel as if they might break open, spray over the walls and windows, the lamps and shades, the dresser, small comb, the mirror and cards, the call button, electric bed, leftover breakfast, bathrobe, hearing aid, radio, over everything, blasting and reckless like an unattended fire hose, a catastrophe of magnanimous proportion, and we would all say, "how are we going to clean this up?" when suddenly the room would roar into sky and ocean, animal clouds whooshing by, and in a moment of complete surprise, up he would step onto the horizon, vanishing into the vault of heaven behind.

"Get me a gun," he says, moving his fingers as if speaking in sign. "Please. This is so bad. Help me."

when mom goes

sometimes my mom has to go away to visit her mother,
who lives in detroit, michigan. my dad doesn't like it when
she goes away. he sort of dims down like he is a light switch,
the kind with the dial. he turns way down when she leaves,
like maybe from a million watts to 40 watts; he is still a bulb,
but we can't read as clearly around him.

the missing of my mother for us kids is around cooking and
eating and getting ready for church on time. when she is away,
there really isn't that much to eat anymore. my father doesn't
know about turning on the stove and cooking up a bunch of
stuff from boxes and all. he just knows one thing: how to make
jellyfish sitting in water—although that's not the real name for
them. most grown-ups call them poached eggs. we kids think
they look and taste a whole lot more like jellyfish. there is no
getting around it, jellyfish for dinner unless some nice neighbor
comes over with a dish.

thing is he looks like a real weirdo standing over the stove with
those huge fingers that kind of collapse the egg instead of
break it. we all hover around watching the birth of the jellyfish,
see little pieces of them rise to the surface, little white globs
that look like tiny white rivers of pollution, and right there we
start feeling sick. then he gives the call for plates and he
scoops out a jellyfish for each of us. the one relief is that he
doesn't just flop it on the plate and let it slither all around like a
huge open eye; try eating food that is watching you. he toasts
up some bread nice and brown, and flat in the middle goes
the jellyfish. i am always really happy about the bread because

it will soak up most of that white river before you really
know it is there.

my dad should have been a painter, a van gogh or a
michaelangelo, because he can just take a swipe at a
canvas and come up with the most beautiful picture, as
if it has been sitting there all along and all that is needed
is for my dad to free it into the world. he can also just put
paint on things like benches and houses or fences that run
along the side of the driveway to keep you driving straight
when you go to the store.

one morning when mom flies off to detroit, my dad has all
these chores to do and he thinks about some help coming
from us girls since we are just hanging around like a little
gang waiting for something to happen. so he finds us all
some clothes with holes and stains in them that don't matter
anymore, and we each get our own brush to do some
painting. of course, he does most of the job, but my sisters
and i put a little paint on the fence and then some on each
other and some on the lawn so it looks like the grass has
gray hair, which is what my father says now and then, that we
are making his hair gray, except not from paint but from being
too much around him all at once. he gives us a laugh after
he says that, a huge one with his teeth, gold specks and all,
and then he dabs a little blip on all our noses so we look like
clowns getting ready for the circus, which is what the next
morning turns into, let me tell you.

during the night i guess what happens is that dad can't sleep
because he misses mom, so he gets up and decides to paint

the living room. i guess he just goes to town, not in the car but in his head, and finishes the whole room in no time flat. since he is such a clean man, he makes that room look like nothing has happened in there since the day before. then he needs to take a little nap, which he certainly deserves, since he hasn't been sleeping.

in the meantime, my sisters and i wake up and want to be all dressed for church early for a change to surprise him, because usually when it comes to going to church with mom gone someone always has an instant breakfast pancake on her lap or syrup on the lacy part of her dress collar. so we get all dressed in the exact outfits mom has hanging on the door knobs, complete with white tights and gloves with the little pearls on the cuffs that you can play with when the sermon gets too long. then, not knowing any different because we sleep at night, we go into the living room and for some reason end up leaning against the wall.

well, when dad gets up and sees that we are all dressed so nicely, he says, "don't you all look pretty. turn around and let me get the whole view," which we do all together and he gives a scream like he does when he stubs his toe on the bed. apparently, from his description, there is more paint on us than he put on the wall, though i can't imagine how that can be, seeing the size of us all together doesn't come near beating the wall. anyway, we all have to fish around in our closets for other dresses to wear. by the end of it we look okay and finally head off to church, leaving our painty dresses soaking in some stuff in the garage.

Conversation: II

Cathy: And then there is the story about the moose

Joan: The one in Canada, on his vacation, by that lake with all the wooden boats and cottages

Cathy: Yeah, he said he was taking its picture and he startled it, and it turned on him and charged

Mom: Oh, you know he always exaggerated. I'm not so sure there was really a moose at all. He loved a good story

Cathy: Yes, Mom, it was a moose he said, and it chased him through the trees, huffing and puffing like it was going to kill him or something

Mom: Who was huffing and puffing, your father? He was probably smoking a cigarette, too, hanging it out of his mouth, you know how he did that

Cathy: No, the moose, it made a huge noise like maybe grunting. Yeah, that's what Dad would have said, a huge grunt chasing him through the night

Polly: It couldn't have been night if he was taking a picture

Cathy: Okay, it was day, and he was taking a picture of the moose and it turned and chased him

Joan: No, that's not the whole story. He wasn't taking a picture, he was taking a video with one of those little old 8-mm cameras, and the whole thing is documented. There's a movie somewhere

Cathy: So he was taking a picture of the ground moving under his feet as the moose chased him

Polly: Yeah, that's all the movie shows, him being chased by something

Dream   *In my dream, God proposes a deal.*
I can have my father back, he will actually be released
immediately, can walk down heaven's stairway and
into my room if I like, but I must give up my mother.
She will have to take her turn being dead now.

Disease-Man

You've been here a long time. Don't you want to go home? The man across the way speaks like a bird. Beak up and flop. Only another six days until they come. I miss the tree in the back years ago I swept everything up and mainly so. Do you know what I mean? And where did your mother go? Where did she go?

Mama Bear, where you are?

Is this the way it is?   No bone crushing.   No cascade of grief. Just a long horn.   And another thing: you knitting in the evening, the click of the needles like a metronome.

And sleep came easily   The click click of the needles

And sleep overcoming me   As I tried to beat back that giant wing

Now is the opening up

Pause between space

the resting place.   *Where are the children? Please*

Since birth, the tally up has been listening

Take me with you

Before I got here.

So now where?   *For God's sake*

I'll never

Get right right   At least now

Call my wife and tell her I'll be late for dinner   Under the bed

death carving a tunnel

Mama Bear, I love you

THE THINKING BRAIN

Many brainless, simple creatures have a nervous system that helps keep them alive by allowing recognition between foe and food or fight and flight. Even the single-celled ameba, which doesn't have a true nervous system, is able to react to certain stimuli, such as light and, quite possibly, even pain. A worm has a nerve network in the center of a primitively developed brain that runs the full length of its body.

When we pull a finger away from a burning fire, we make an involuntary, or unthinking, movement that is controlled by local centers in a nervous system, much like the worm. But a human can also make voluntary movements that are controlled by a thinking brain.

A human's brain seems to be made up of groups of outgrowths, all fulfilling different organizing functions but all housed in the skull. Under the back of the brain is the cerebellum, which helps to regulate the way we walk. If we had only half a cerebellum, we could not walk straight. The upper main part of the brain, the cerebrum, makes up nine-tenths of the brain's total bulk. Its outer layer, called the cortex, has a gray, wrinkled, rubbery surface, unlike the smooth cortex of lower animals. In general, the more wrinkled a creature's cortex, the more intelligent the creature seems to be. The cerebrum seems to be responsible for what we call reasoning, feeling, and will. Parts of it also control our actions.

The cerebrum is made up of two hemispheres. The left one controls muscle movements on the right side of the body, while the right one controls the left side. In healthy people, nerve messages travel along the brain's nerve fibers, which cross each other in an oblong organ situated where the brain joins the spine.

The thinking brain can be compared to a submarine commander. The eye (periscope) sends its messages to the brain (the commander), whose judgment controls the movements of the limbs (the sailors).

If you burn your finger on a match, you do not have to think about what to do. But if you meet an angry bull in a field midway between two gates, you must make a snap decision. In such a tight spot, the brain works at remarkable speed. And when you decide which way to run, nerve impulses from brain to leg muscles move at almost 300 mph. Even the commander of the most modern submarine could not change course half as quickly as you would start to run.

Abridged from *Life and Its Marvels: Plant, Animal, Human.*

Part Two

His Wife

In the picture she is standing on the deck of a ferryboat in New York harbor, wearing a black half coat with big black buttons, a white scarf wrapped around her head. It is cold. Her arm is looped through his so that there is little separation between them, just a small patch of blue background and the top of a building on the New York skyline. He is, as usual, towering above, wrapped in a khaki overcoat that is buttoned to just below the neck so you can see his tie. Both hands are in his pockets, and the side of him that faces her is cast in shadow, her shadow, seeming to block the sun, if only for a moment, from shining between them.

My father met my mother, his wife, on a mixed-up blind date. She and her best friend were to have drinks with Dad and his best friend. They all met in some ritzy hotel in New York, all sparkle and expectations, ordered up martinis and rum punches, and then "oh, really'ed" and "you don't say'ed" until someone had the bright idea to switch the seating chart so that my father and mother could sit together. From then on, the evening changed to "me, too's" and "I'd like that's," and it was apparent the pairings were better suited.

After that, they spent lots of time swinging around New York's high society, checking out cool parties with low lights, music, and dancing, all decked out in mink coats and black jackets. Dad was quite a handsome man—"stunning," people would say—and Mom a beauty who looked like she should have been sauntering down a promenade in Paris. My parents just naturally looked good together, and everyone told them that's how it should be, the two of them happily-ever-after.

But they decided to play it cool. They each dated other people, too, during a five-year period, maybe just to compare the goods. Maybe Mom wanted to slip into the shadows so she could think more about this towering man who seemed to adore her. Dad needed to decide if he was really ready to give up the life of a bachelor.

Mom threw herself into her work at Lord and Taylor, and Dad steamed off on the *Queen Mary* for Europe, which for him was a dream come true. I'll bet he wished he could have been a little kid so he could get one of those plastic ocean-liner pins to wear on his jacket lapel. No doubt he tried to talk his way into the captain's bridge to see how the ship was run, which, of course, he knew by heart as he had read every book about her. Years later, when he bought his first sailboat, just a blue sunfish, he named it the *Queen Mary*. The name was almost longer than the boat.

When he got to Europe, he toured all around with his sister Barbie, seeing places that for years he had only hoped to see. But while he was having the time of his life, he was lonely and sad with no one by his side except for his sister, whom he loved, of course, but couldn't live with anymore.

Then one night in Venice he became ill and disoriented, got up in the middle of the night and shaved off his moustache, which had probably been a real nuisance if he was vomiting a lot. In the morning, sick and yellow in the face, he looked in the mirror and decided he needed someone to take care of him. He knew of only two people in his life he would like to do that: his mother and his wife, though she wasn't "his wife" yet.

With that decided, he enjoyed the rest of the trip, lost his mind at all the cathedrals, and came home. He called Mom and asked if they could start some serious dating, like headed-for-marriage dating, which they did, and were engaged in August when Dad slammed a beautiful ring on Mom's finger one carriage-ride evening in Central Park.

A glitch in the works really revealed the "his wife" part. Shortly after their engagement, Mom was offered a buyer's job at

Lord and Taylor. The management expected her to work after she was married, even after she had kids, which, of course, she was going to have, didn't everyone? She said yes to the working part and suggested to Dad that a nanny might be in order to take care of the children so she could fly off to places around the world, looking at fancy clothes and feeling the fabric. Dad, though, was a real stickler for tradition. He felt it was the job of the husband to provide the money, and the job of the wife to provide the family. "No wife of mine is going to work," he told her one dark night. "You tell them no to the job."

Then he didn't call her for three days, probably to let her know he was serious, no fooling around. Finally, she called him to meet her in a bar for a drink to help her say it to them.

Which she did. In the saddest voice, as if someone were squeezing it out of her, she said no to the job.

She had to stay home and be his wife because that's the way things were back then, no choice, just a bunch of roles, and she'd better play her part. That's how the whole family thing started. They got married at a big cathedral in New York, with lots of very tall people down front, Dad's family, like him, all tall and hard to see through, so when Mom came down the aisle it was hard for her to see what her life was going to be like with everyone in the way.

Though he was strict with her at the beginning about the job, he adored her. Without her, he was lost. Later on, when he was lost for real, she was his salvation.

When Dad got so sick, Mom had to take care of him because that is the obligation of love. Sometimes, I know, she just wanted to up and pack her bags, land a taxi, and hit the road to somewhere far, far away. Once when I was talking to her on the phone, trying to find out how he was doing without having to talk to him (sometimes I would hang up the phone when he answered; I hate myself for that now), she just broke into tears and no words, and

I had to listen to the flicking of tissue long distance and not ask what's wrong, because I knew, and not ask anything else because what was there to say at that point.

She said he just followed her around all day, even sometimes when she had to go to the bathroom. It seemed he needed to know where she was so he could be where she was. If she went too far away, he couldn't remember she was there. It's like she was his memory, and when she left, it did, too. Sometimes I would imagine what they must have looked like in the house, Mom walking around trying to do stuff and Dad right there behind her, so close that when she stopped he rammed into her back.

I used to think, in a silly sort of way, about kangaroos and how they carry their kids around in a pouch. I thought, since Dad was acting so much like a kid at this point, too bad Mom didn't have a pouch. Then she could just whoosh him in there and zip it up like a purse for a few minutes of peace and quiet.

In the end I think if he could have, my dad would have waltzed my mother right into death with him.

So she could continue being his wife.

Deaf Man

One day my dad went deaf, let go of sounds, just plain and simple couldn't hear anymore. We'd have to turn the TV up so loud that I thought the people on the screen were in the living room. It would make me jump around in my head and feel like a crazy person. He was always asking us to repeat ourselves and then we would, trying to say what we'd said a little louder without sounding too annoyed, which we were because who likes to keep hearing themselves say the same thing over and over? Then he would get mad and say forget it, no matter, like he wasn't important enough to deal with anyway, so then we would have to convince him that yes, he was important, and he'd say could you speak a little louder, and then we'd be yelling at him how important he was and pretty soon the whole room would blur and sound like we were all insane, which we were by that point.

One night I was sitting in the car with him waiting for my mom to come back from buying something in the 24-hour store. She was taking so long I thought she might have been hijacked to another country; I hated it when she just seemed to disappear into the night. Anyway, my dad and I were talking. For some reason I was in the front seat and he was sitting in the back seat, probably because he had more leg room and he could spread out those knees and let them breathe back there without any fuss. Now with the deafness I had to look right at him when I was speaking or he wouldn't catch a thing.

Out the window I could see the moon rising, and I knew that the moon was a favorite thing of his, so I stopped talking and watched it come up, so lovely on the horizon, all orange and hopeful. Then I said, without turning around, just sort of to my arm that was holding my head, I said, "Isn't that something," almost whispered it so I could barely hear it. I didn't really say it to my dad, I just said it to the faintest ear around, but after a moment, I could hear him smile, hear the muscles in his face move into a wide grin, and he said, very softly, too, "Yes, it is." I looked back at his smiling face, at all the free space around him, and I knew that by the time my mother came bounding back to the car to tell us how all the people in there had kept her waiting, he would be deaf again.

Conversation: III

Polly: The first night we went, the room was very cold and there were no flowers

Joan: And that flight trying to get to the funeral. They couldn't find the lock for the hatch door. I called from the air

Polly: It was very real to me, the nitty-gritty of it. We used to do Dad's laundry. He always wore those big, blue terry-cloth bibs, and the kids put them on, wearing them like capes. On my kids they were Superman capes and on Dad they were bibs. I can remember changing his diapers. He was so big you needed someone to hold him. Somehow that man held on to his dignity. Even through that, he did it

Cathy: I never saw that

Polly: After Dad died, I wasn't at peace with him. I just didn't get why he wouldn't tell me where he was and, I don't know, how I was supposed to get on with my life. It seemed there was just an eternity ahead. Then I took that vacation with Doug and the boys to the coast. I was really quite despairing. One morning I got up early to take a walk on the beach. I spoke out loud to him. I said, "Dad, you just have to tell me what to do." Well, you know how people hear voices? I heard his. "Take care of the living," Dad said to me. "Quit thinking about the dead." It was sunrise. I went back to the condo we were staying in and got my family up and took care of them. It seemed like for years I had been asking for some kind of connection, and it was almost as if I could hear him saying, "Enough. Just take care of the living."

Mom: He died before he was ready to, and in some state of confusion that he was working through, and it was taking time. He wasn't ready. But the night before he died I was there, and he looked beyond me and he was smiling. I was sitting next to the bed and he was smiling, and he had such a look of peace on his face. He was seeing something. Yes, I got a lot of peace from that. The next day I was going to have to sign an irrevocable trust, and the next day he died. He was at peace

Polly: I remember saying something like, "I don't know what to do." I was sitting in the tub talking to you, Mom, thinking I can't stand this conversation because she is talking about feeding tubes, and I thought, dignity is big with me and that would be horrible, so much has been taken from him. And I said on the phone to you

Mom: You wanted

Polly: Do I need to come down, I said

Mom: And I said, no, you don't need to

Polly: I remember just sitting in the bath. It was unbearable about the feeding tube. I prayed then. I said, "Please, God, do something. Don't let him suffer the indignity of the feeding tube." Of course what I meant was make him eat. And so the next morning when Doug came and told me Dad had died, I had enormous guilt—that had been the only answer to that prayer

Cathy: Wait, back up, back up

Polly: I remember praying that prayer. Then I remember calling you, and then Doug came over to the church. Isn't that funny, I saw Doug in the parking lot, and I thought, why isn't he at work? I thought he had said *his* father died. "I'm sorry, your mother called," he said. "Your father died"

Mom: You remember that moment forever. You never forget

Cathy: You left the message on my machine

Mom: I regret he left that first nursing home. He had such a struggle after that. When he faced any kind of change

Polly: I remember driving you guys to the airport and having to walk onto the plane with you and settling him into the chair and having to turn and walk away

Mom: It wasn't yours to do or not to do. It was my decision. We did the best we could at the time

Polly: I always thought Howard was his guardian angel. So why did we move him

Mom: I had to get back. I had to make some kind of permanent decision. It was just one of those situations that looked like the best thing to do, and they had assured me they could handle him, so we did all we could do

Cathy: Then he wound up in a psychiatric hospital, and they took his watch away. Then he got sent to another place for an evaluation

Mom: I don't know

Joan: And then, what was the last place called

Mom: But think of all those people who visited him often at the end; his friendship was so important to them

Cathy: There is no telling which way it will go

Joan: First Marion. Didn't she get really bad at the end? Curl up like a child? Then Dad. When did it start

Mom: And his mom and dad, though back then it just seemed to be old age

Cathy: When did Dad start getting bad? When was he not sick

Mom: Eight years, nine . . . he changed slowly. There were still many moments, right up to the end. The last time I took him in the car . . . we just sat there, didn't go far. Suddenly he turned to me and with brilliant clarity said, "Mama Bear, how are you getting along"

Cathy: He knew . . . something was there, in the air somewhere, pieces of his life still floating by. He could grab one

Mom: Like his whole life was in him busting to get out. He was everywhere and nowhere at the same time. Like all our lives were in there. He had us

Joan: He still does

WONDERS OF LIFE AND DEATH

All highly developed animals, even if they escape death from accident, must die sooner or later. While many evolved creatures have extremely long life spans, their time on earth is always measured.

But few species rival man's capacity to live a possible 120 years. A man can walk his dog along a beautiful sandy beach, but he cannot walk the same dog throughout his lifetime. Instead he must walk six different dogs to equal his life span. A man can crouch and capture a small frog skimming the surface of a pond, but he cannot keep that frog for more than one-tenth of his life. He would have to capture ten frogs successively if he wanted one with him every day of his life. However, if a man in his 120th year leans over to scoop up a small turtle from a mud bank, the turtle would have 30 more years to live.

Unfortunately, few animals living in the wild actually reach their life span due to accidents, predators, and disease. However, if held captive in a zoo with regularly provided food and care, these animals may well live out their life-span potential, but, most certainly, it would be a life without freedom or purpose.

Abridged from *Life and Its Marvels: Plant, Animal, Human.*

Disease-Man

Yes, I have a lovely wife, Judy. She comes to visit me every day, but sometimes she's late or forgets about it, and I wind up in the hospital begging for food. We are going to the country today. Our honeymoon.

God damn it, leave me alone. If you're going to take one arm, take them both. I'm unemployed. Just pull them out the ends of my elbows. Then get me a gun, for God's sake, can't someone get me a gun? I can't take much more of this. I know what's happening, I know my mind is going numb. Jason, Jason, where's Jason? He'll need a walk or else he'll pee all over the floor. Then I'll have to give him a bath. Somebody get the leash, he's out front waiting for me. I'll take him into the woods.

Marion and I and Barbie used to go to the cottage each summer. Dad would come on weekends, and I'd see the *Segwin* speed across the lake, people spilling over the decks. I'd watch until the steam hung faintly in the sky, only a wisp remaining, like just the smallest death, and I'd walk the four miles back to the cottage, where dinner was always waiting.

I've seen Marion here many times. She comes at night up the side of the bed, telling me about the demon inside. It's her demon, too; she died from it. She is here warning me to step away, move off into the water. The night she died, Jason moaned her passing, saw her swimming above the bed.

Some Sort of Commotion

Traffic on U.S. 1 is stopped completely. "Bridge is up," Mom says. A cat lounges in the window of the dark blue Dodge Shadow ahead, stretching its front paws as it gives a long, slow yawn. The bumper sticker on the car's trunk reads, "I brake for Siamese."

"Those are weird cats," I say, picking at my big toe. "They look kind of evil, up to something. You know, sinister."

"All cats look like that. Remember Chuck?"

"Oh, my God. I forgot about him. He was a cool cat, come on."

"If you call lining up lizards' tails on the patio cool. I think it's evil."

"He was just trying to show off. They were his prizes."

"Every morning your father had to go out there and pick them up. I just stood in the bedroom and screamed."

"You screamed?"

"Well, I yelled quietly."

"He was abused you know. I found him with his legs tied to his collar. It was so sad. I don't remember what you did with him."

"The animal shelter. Polly was allergic."

"Oh, yeah, right. That was it for Chuck."

Out the window I see an aluminum mast slide between the raised pieces of concrete. A man in a yellow windbreaker and black cap hugs the mast with one arm while tugging at a halyard with the other. Another man, shirtless and sunburned, glides by at the helm, waving a two-fingered thank-you to the guy in the little house on stilts. A brief pause, then the concrete folds into a road again.

"The Ashleys were asking about you. Hope you'll stop for a visit while you're here. Swim laps in their pool."

"How are they?"

"Her mother just died, you knew that. And he's better. Still on the oxygen, but mobile. Brings it to the bridge games."

"He's been so sick, it's amazing he's still alive."

"Oh, he was clinically dead several times. It's all her, she does so much, waits on him hand and foot."

We start moving and speed past bulldozers and cranes, huge piles of dirt and sand.

"Whenever I come here, something is different. What are they building now?"

"Blockbuster Video and a CVS. No, not CVS, Eckerd's. Actually, it will be more convenient. I won't have to drive to the end of North Dixie Highway."

In the distance, a traffic light turns yellow, then red. Mom pulls into the left-hand turning lane, waits for the green arrow, and then scoots onto River Road.

We fly easily along, passing decent homes framed by palm trees and motorboats. Huge sprays of roses, rhododendron, hibiscus, and azaleas cram the gardens. A small pond with ducks appears.

"See the loons?" Mom asks.

"Those aren't loons, they're brown. Loons are black and white. Red eye."

"Those are loons."

"From Canada, this far south? I thought just to North Carolina or something."

"For the winter. Then they go home."

We turn a corner and slow down to let a car finish backing into the street. Through the trees I can see quick flashes of water and light. "How's Dad?"

Blinker-blink and we turn onto North Victory Lane, slow down considerably, and creep towards the end of the road, pulling into the cement driveway of the house my parents have lived in for five years. It's cedar-shingled, a very chic kind of bungalow-looking place all tucked into bushes and palm trees, there but not there at the same time. The thick, chunky shingles look like huge pieces of a Hershey bar.

"You tell me."

Jason, my golden retriever who lives here now, sways around the corner with a tennis ball in his mouth, followed quickly by my father, who never lets him out of his sight.

"Jas!" I clapclap, and he comes bounding over, puts two muddy paws on my airport clothes, and noses the ball into my hand. "Hey, bud!" I drum on his sleek chest and then throw the ball towards the fence. He flops after it, mouths it on the first bounce, then circles back, grunting and talking, wanting to play. Dad stands three feet away, smiling at the dog he adores.

"Hi, Dad." I wrap my arms around his belly and kiss the button on his shirt.

"Hello, daughter," he says, patting the side of my face, then backs away. "Hello, you," he says to my mother, putting his hand on her shoulder, closing the door to the car. "How was the trip?"

"Slow," she says. "The bridge was up. Huge schooner. You would have loved it, dear."

"Yeah, Dad, it was beautiful. So high in the water the guy steering looked like he might step off onto the bridge and have a chat."

"No captain should abandon ship," he says with a smile. He opens the trunk and grabs my suitcase. "I'll put this in your room. Mama Bear, what's for lunch?"

"Oh, anything. I'll look in the refrigerator. How about open-faced cheese and tomato?"

Dad walks towards the front door. With one quick pull, he jams the door open with the suitcase, swings his left foot around, and disappears into the blue portal. "Sounds divine," he yells from inside. The door shushhh-click-clinks behind him.

I sling my brown leather bag over my shoulder. "He seems pretty good."

"Today," she nods, shifting and lifting her way inside.

After lunch, I drag a chaise lounge into a patch of sun by the pool, pulling it close to the edge so I can dangle my feet. Dad is skimming bugs and little tree-things from the top of the water. He looks like a giant sunflower, bent in earnest, chest bare except for a few long and curly hairs that hang on for dear life.

Dad, you should bulk up, I think, get some of the powdered stuff that tastes like yeast. "The pool looks nice," I say. "How do you keep it so clean?"

"It's how I stay in the sun without guilt. Do a little everyday. Besides, you know your mother. She won't go in the pool if it's not clean. Screams about the bugs." He knocks the skimmer on the pavement, and a stringy piece of palm tree falls out.

"She doesn't go in much anyway, does she?"

"Oh, she'll get her toe in a bit, then sometimes up to her waist." He strains to reach clear across the pool to where I am sitting, holding the skimmer in one hand as if offering me a ride in the basket, then lets it plunk and sink into the water, heaves it up. "Won't get her hair wet." He smiles, glunks a bunch of stuff on the cement, hits the scooper-thing a few times, hangs it up on the wall. Then he bends over a white, plastic bucket-plug, pulls it out, dumps the sludge behind the sidewall, and replaces it. "Promised your mother I'd check the dryer. Last week a snake crawled up the vent and died in a load of whites. Got to cement holes in the lawn. Get some boots." He reaches down and scratches our dog's ear, rubbing his thumb over its smooth velvet interior. Jason rolls onto his back, feet sticking straight up. "Come on, boy," he coos, and they disappear together towards the garage.

I sit up in my chair, reach back, and lower it to the all-the-way-down position. Placing my extra pair of sunglasses over the pair I already have on, I stare up at the sky.

Mom pokes her head out of the sliding glass door. "I'm in the middle of something. Could you run to Publix and get some sugar?"

"Yeah, five more minutes? Till more clouds come?" She waves a white hand. Settling back I watch a plane enter my line of vision. It is so high there is no sound, only the tiniest movement as it abracadabras in whiffs of cloud smoke, leaving behind it a wake like unraveled stitches from a knitting needle. It is impossible to imagine 200 people sitting on the tip of my finger, drinking martinis and eating peanuts, reading *Newsweek* magazine. I spend all my flying time trying to stay alive, either by keeping the plane up (leaning forward during takeoff) or by picturing myself walking away from the inevitable crash, pulling others from the fiery hulk as I pass. I read about a guy who did this. As the plane nosed down, he visualized leaving the scene as if he were stepping away from a party, all very civilized and safe and slightly drunk, so that when the plane did crash, he just unbuckled his seat belt and tiptoed through tons of dead bodies. Like Jeff Bridges in that movie where he and some little kid are bushwhacking out of one disaster and into another; Bridges then spends the rest of the movie trying to die because he hadn't died. But I am a hero, saving 20 or 30 passengers by ripping the escape hatch from its hinges (I *always* sit in the emergency exit row), helping them onto the blow-up-doll slide that whooshes them to safety. After that, TV appearances, lectures, medals . . . maybe a call from the president. Arrival at my destination is never simple. I have always just escaped death's clutches by a simple act of grace.

Some sort of commotion is coming from inside the house. I wrap a bath towel with a red *Z* on it around my waist, pick up the blue-and-white plastic glass we used to use on the boat, which still smells faintly of vodka, and oou-oou-hot-hot across the burning pavement. Dad is sitting in one of the ivy-patterned, wrought-iron dining room chairs, wearing a shirt around his face like a veil. He looks like a weird Egyptian pharaoh. "What's going on?" I plunk down in one of the swivel chairs and stare at Dad.

Huge sigh from Mom. "Your father wants to get the mail and he can't find his hat, so he wants to try this, but . . . ," she trails off.

"The doctor told me I should never go outside without a hat on because of the skin cancer." Dad stands up suddenly, and the shirt slides to the ground. He reaches down and grabs it, slams it back on his head, and stands at attention.

"But you were just outside in the sun without it," I try.

"The doctor told me never," he scolds.

"How about if I get the mail?" I ask, heading for the front door.

"I'm not helpless, you know. I can walk to the mailbox, for God's damn sake. Jason, come on," he commands, and out the door they go, Dad holding the crumpled shirt on his head like ice on a bump.

Mom wipes her hands on her green-and-white-striped apron, then moves to the counter and begins to measure out cups of milk. I get in the silver Honda Accord and drive to the store for the sugar. Overhead, a sudden hurry of blue, then dark clouds weave and threaten rain. I think about all the injustice in my life.

Publix is the epitome of why I hate grocery shopping altogether and particularly why I hate it in Florida. Old people seem piled double-decker to keep me from maneuvering down the aisle for a simple box of sugar, which is hard to find because of all the health-care products jamming the aisles, rows and rows of Pampers, pantiliners for women, tubes for God knows what, pills, pulleys.

"Paper or plastic, ma'am?"

"I don't need anything," I reply, pushing $1.20 at the "We Try" button and shifting out the door. As I approach the parking spot, I see my reflection in the hood of my father's car and realize he still waxes it.

When I get back, the house is quiet and cool; I move into its shadows. Jason is lying on the white tile in the front hall. He raises his head, the tags on his collar jing-jingling, then kleepumps back down with a thump. The door to my parent's bedroom is closed.

As I round the corner, I hear whispering, small huffs of conversation coming from outside. Dad is sitting cross-legged on the patio talking to a ficus tree, leaning in as if to hear every word. He looks oddly peaceful after the earlier blow, as if the tree is telling him the secret to surviving this storm.

I go into the bathroom, close the door, and stare into the mirror to see if I am tan yet.

That night we have a huge downpour, and the next morning there are millions of frogs floating belly-up in the pool. Dad is already out there when I get out of bed, scooping them into the skimmer as if on some sort of rescue. The yellow bodies line the patio like about-to-be water toys, and I wonder if he will pick one up and croak-croak it around the sides of the pool like my little nephews do, pretending it is a vibrant and living creature, pretending he is, too.

Disease-Man

I've got to get to work. Sam is waiting. 9:00 sharp. I have a job. Judy, where is Judy? And my suit. Linda is waiting for me. Linda, I'm coming. I'll be there soon. For God's sake, I'll miss the train.

The ghost on the wall. I see it riding across right there. Linda, I'll miss my train. Judy, where are the kids? They are watching me, those who have already died. I feel them brushing up against my legs, the shock of news, the paper sliding across the seat, and who the hell is this telling me something? What do you want, woman? What? I can't understand you.

Where are my slippers? I want to leave right now. Where is my father? Dad, call Dad at the mill. He is the vice president there. Make him do something. Bring me home. Mother, wind the clock, for heaven's sake, can't you hear it is dying? Judy, where is my wife? I am going to miss the train. I can't even see you, whoever you are. I don't know what you have come to tell me. This ride to the city every day. I'm exhausted, my bones are calling me, something white keeps flashing on the ceiling. For God's sake, what have they done with the sky?

One of the women in here has long feet. Probably nine or ten inches. No arch, just straight flat. So flat they suck the ground and make noise. Not just pounding noise that makes me jump but cracking noise as if something is breaking on the inside. They must be model feet, and she is trying them on for some company

to sell.
Either that
or she is
mean,
coming in
here at
night with
all the
noise
before her.
Flatfoots
need
forgiveness.
    I have
no idea
what I'm
going to
do with
my life. It's
terribly
cold this
morning. I
suppose I
should be
grateful it's
not winter
and
snowing
or blowing
so hard the
windows
rattle like
the lungs
of
someone
about to
die. That
happens
with
tubercu-
losis. It's a
purr-rattle,
purr-rattle.
At first I
do not
understand
what it is.
Like
listening to
a rattle
snake in
the
country.
It's not
possible it
would be
what it
truly is. It's
like the
sounds
here.
    The
sick
helicopters,
the
fuppfupp
fuppfupp
of a
nervous
breakdown,
and the
patient lies
coma-like,
listening to
the rattle
of his
bones.

The Last Time

Because Dad wanted so badly to leave with us when it came time to go after our visits at the nursing home, the attendant would strap him into a blue plastic chair, tie him in like a hostage—three black ties holding him tight, so he couldn't move, so he wouldn't hurt anyone, so he would behave and sit still.

That is my last image of my father, him in that chair, waving good-bye to me. If I look at that memory as it seemed that day, I can't move. But if I tip it a bit, as if holding a small mirror in the light, maybe then I can see that it isn't really my father at all but a little boy playing spaceman, the chair his station inside an enormous rocket that will carry him away. He is waving to the cheering crowd as he prepares to blast off.

Whist

Late shadow moon's toothing

           long night   alley-wide

Patching bluedot rose dusking   yellow finger's evil side.

    Geese of flocking   small stacks

       spotted bellies fire-tracks

honkingback   thunderclouds

   slivergraycovershrouds.

Lonely figure dropping back

        eyes stare   a bending there

ear shoulder eyes close   a smoking gun's final load.

    What's it like, death's road?   the wholepictureovertold

circle backing half a rack

          a foreign cry

          black.

100 miles an hour

my dad is always being touched by something, as if he is
way connected to his feelings and they are going 100 miles
an hour down the road, like his heart is bigger than a normal
heart or maybe he even has two. sometimes i see him just
staring out the window with his finger running above his lip like
he is checking on his shaving job, and i know some feeling
stuff is vrooming up inside him. usually there isn't anything
out that window that i can see, but i think that he uses the
window for a resting place to kind of calm down and take
a deep breath before going out the door to work or to the
hardware store, so that he just doesn't go to pieces, which
is not what my dad should be doing since he has to look like
a dad who knows where the duct tape is or the nails are. so
he plants himself at that window with his eyes so that he can
just see where his heart is going without any interruptions.
sometimes he gets lucky and there is a real bird out there
for him to see. he looks around the room and calls over to
anyone who happens to be nearby, "come see the bird,"
and he usually points out something incredible like the little
feathers on the top of the cardinal's head. then he looks a
little longer, just bugs his eyes out closer to the scene, gives
a big sigh that includes rolling his shoulders, and turns away
and moves on to the next activity, which for my dad could be
just about anything.

like flowers. he can really grow them. he has this incredible
garden at the foot of the lawn that looks like a greenhouse
without the glass, like the kind you see on tv or in books.

he plants them all from seeds, reading the directions carefully and doing it exactly his way anyway. they always come up beautifully, as if he spends his whole life in the earth. the colors look like a rainbow blend, as if that is a type of flower. the flowers are different heights at different times, kind of like children, and he lines them up the same way children get lined up for picture-taking, with the tall guys in the back, mediums in the middle, and shorties down front. it's like the flowers are his family. sometimes when my mom and sisters and i come home from somewhere, we find him sitting right in the middle of his family, smoking a cigarette. when we drive up the driveway, he throws a huge wave of an arm up to us, pushes himself tall, and comes to help us—his family that lives outside of the garden with no earth on our feet— carry in whatever we bought at the store.

to get back to his heart, things aren't going too well at times. his heart just isn't a good one, doesn't work right. it goes on the blink and just does what it pleases, or it pounds out of his chest, goes fifty times faster than normal, as if he is running a race. it beatbeatbeatbeats like a hand pounding from his chest to get out, over and over, pounding on the door screaming, "let me out." when this happens, he takes small blue pills and a huge gulp of water and lies down with his hands on top of his chest, tapping back and forth like the wings of a butterfly getting ready to go, which at times he had to do, go somewhere to take care of his body.

when one of my sisters is only two weeks old, my dad goes to the hospital and just lies on his back for three weeks. then he goes to some guy and is cured for good because someone rubs his back a lot and gives him a million heating pads a day, which for dad is the best since he loves the heat—"please someone turn up the thermostat, i'm freezing"—so being at this place is like summer forever without the sun. the only bad thing about this place is all the white gauze that has to be wrapped around him so his back stays in place. when we visit, we stand outside the window and wave, all holding hands and looking at him just lying there in what looks like a dead body that can't move, with a head that is smiling away and wants to get up and dance.

another thing about his body is that it loves to drink milk. for breakfast he makes that instant stuff, and we can hear the spoon clinking in the glass all the way upstairs in our beds. he gets up at the crack of dawn before most people have even considered waking and clinkclinkclink we hear through the darkness, and i can see in my mind the long silver spoon reaching down to all that gunk that collects at the bottom of the glass. his favorites are vanilla and chocolate but forget the strawberry, nobody likes that.

he drinks a ton of milk morning, noon, and night, just glubs it down, and i'm not talking that skim-blue milk that i drink, he drinks the stuff that tastes like cream, which you want to hold in your mouth for a long time, not spit out. he isn't fat, so he doesn't have to worry, he just loads it all in like he is storing up for a war or something.

he stands at the window to drink it, in his blue or gray or sometimes striped suit, and stares out at whatever is moving. he enjoys looking out at the morning that is starting to come from behind the trees; he loves to watch the mist rise off the grass, the way it glistens silver and shivers a little like it is cold, and then the day will spray ahead really fast, get light and right into things, no fooling around. he likes having another day come so he can walk into it and look at the sky and look at the flowers and be his total self.

apparently the milk, even though it doesn't make him fat, gets into his bones, and he has to have an operation to get it out. his shoulders get stuck, and he can't move his huge arms over his head without some help or else a low moan from his throat and a bad look on his face. some days are pretty bad, and he moves around all stiff like a soldier, the way a soldier moves his whole body at once, not just parts of it, and never looks around or even moves his head, like his neck is so stiff that the option of looking at the whole world is no longer possible, he can only look straight ahead and hope nothing hits him from the side.

off he goes to the hospital where they suck out the milk and loosen him up again so he can be that happy-flappy dad who sometimes looks like a rag doll all hanging about with those stretched-out arms and legs. now at least everything will move the way it is supposed to and the hope is that the milk will just mind its own business and stay in his stomach and not leak out again into the body where it can hurt him.

even before he goes to the hospital because of a body that breaks down sometimes, he goes to the hospital to pick up us kids when we are born. when my mom has me really early in the morning, he stays for a little while to look at me, like i'm a doll or something, and then leaves to go clean things up around the house they live in since i'll need some room to play when i get there. after a while he comes back, and my mom can hear his footsteps coming down the hall, and she probably sees the picture of him in her mind with a big smile and a curly thing of hair around his ear that she will cut when she gets home. he walks into the room and walks straight to the window that looks out on the water and says, "that's the biggest damn freighter i have ever seen," meaning a boat out the window, not me. but then he is at the bed and makes a big ohhhh, she is so beautiful, can i hold her fuss-fuss, and from then on he forgets the freighter and window and walks right over to the bed without another peek outside.

all he can think of for a name is mary, which my mom doesn't think is a great name anyway, but for a person with the last name of smith already, it really is plain and ordinary, which no one wants to be so why start them off on the wrong track with such a dumb name. he keeps saying, "mary, mary," like he's already met her or something, which of course he hasn't because there is no mary except in his mind, but my mom wins and they name me catherine elizabeth, "after the queen," my father says, the queen of england, whom he really likes because he is from canada, which is a little part of england, so i am a queen, and that is that.

in a year, my sister comes along, and he digs up mary again. "mary, mary," he says at my mom, "i want to call her mary," which my mom just doesn't want, and she says, "i want to call her paula." so he says, "but i thought we had agreed on abigail or jennifer," and my mom says she wants paula and he says okay. he is a pretty happy guy when it comes right down to it; he won't hurt a fly or argue too long.

when my last sister comes along, mary pops up again, but this is only after thinking that maybe this one is going to be a boy, which of course will be named derek, after my dad's middle name. that idea goes right out the window when the doctor comes down to the room where my dad waits and says that dad must be doing something wrong since he is getting another girl.

and none of us are named mary.

when my mom comes around from the last baby, after she is done pushing all the stuff out of her stomach, she tells my dad that we need a bigger house with more bedrooms and that dad has to go hunting for houses, not the kind of hunting with animals involved or fishing on the side, but the kind where you are looking really hard for something you want a lot. after that he doesn't spend much time anymore in the hospitals, just in houses where the rest of us are.

Possible Homicide

Eventually it was a matter of life and death, his taking the little blue pills that kept his heart pumping. My mother would line them up in a seven-day, white plastic box, and he'd have to take them every six hours or else, which meant or else he could drop dead. Sometimes my mother would set the alarm, not that she would ever forget, but more because she could get distracted for a moment and it would leap past without her knowing it and everything could be over, because, of course, my father couldn't remember anything by then.

Sometimes, towards the end, my sisters and I talked about wanting to take him to the beach, his favorite place, and just sit with him on the sand. When the timer in our heads went off for his pills, we'd ignore it, just put our arms around him and watch the waves breaking at our feet and be there until we saw his soul jump out and leap into the waves, until he was a free man.

Disease-Man

Howard?

heaven

we spend a lot of time at church since it's the first step to
heaven, or at least that's what they want us to think, those
guys with the robes and scarves hanging on necks. dad always
seems happy here. there is a huge piano in the back that
hangs on forever and makes my insides shake and my feet
buzz like maybe i'm growing or something. mostly this music
plays when people are singing and standing up with books
in their hands and voices zinging around like bees, one here
then there. and the lady way in the back row—i look to see if
her voice got out and floated to the top somewhere. i like the
music and all, but mostly i like the part where we have to all be
quiet together. i especially like kneeling on the squeaking green
bench that we pull down so we don't bop our knees on the
floor. my favorite part is when everyone deep-throats a prayer
and i jam my eyes into my fists looking like i am really getting
into the words and seeing god and all that religious stuff when
really what i am seeing is a million stars right there in back of
my knuckles, a whole universe that is my own. sometimes i
think it is the most beautiful thing i've ever seen.

*onward, christian soldiers, marching as to war, with the cross
of jesus going on before,* my father belts out. we kids get a
break in the middle of church. right before the sermon starts
up and everyone's eyes roll back in their heads, we get let
out and go screaming down the center aisle to sunday school.
*christ, the royal master, leads against the foe; forward into
battle see his banners go!* my dad knows all about that, so
they ask him to teach sunday school, like he is an expert on

the subject, which he probably is. it *is* quite a sight, the whole pack of kids leaning into the back of the church and dad hauling up behind us looking like his head might hit the ceiling or bang on the golden cross we have to worship right before we leave. *gates of hell can never gainst that church prevail; we have christ's own promise, and that cannot fail.* people watch him walk by and they smile, probably glad he is the one taking care of their kids and not them, thinking thank goodness for this man who will give us a break to hear the sermon instead of trying to shushshush everyone up like a little choo-choo train let loose in the pew. *onward, christian soldiers, marching as to war, with the cross of jesus going on before.*

Disease-Man

The sound of that water in the distance, the shush, shush, whoosh, and the feet, running on top, coming to get me, the tiny drops of water and nineteen waterfalls all lit up, that beautiful water moving over the earth, and the girls watching from the window that cold gray day when the arms and the legs of the sky moved and Niagara Falls looked grand from Canada, where we walked when the girls took me on the trip up north.

Murmuring Zephyrs

Tonight's sky's a long argument of wind. A whistle up and listen. Listen to the wind. It's fighting something. Overhead, the moon passes into shadow, an arc slices the night in half. Black geese, firebellies, honk and kick through a slickening sky. This is it. I know, this is it. Or maybe yesterday—the bird passed on the road, bowing its head to death and the unshakable whiff of pain oh pain, please turn this into something I can hear.

Where is everyone?

Call in the love. I need to be reminded to live. Nothing is more than this, the light spilling off your face, your hands reaching up to touch mine in prayer.

I'd like to die a little while,

pull your name through

ME

clean   the   inside   of this flute

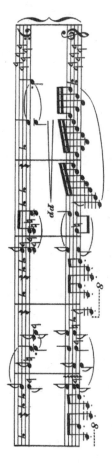    

I would	apart, take	around it.	I see	outside,	through
die today,	out the	I can feel	shadows	and I hear	the
if I could.	snake	the snake	of birds	them	ground.
Just let go.	that's	that has	on the	down in	
Pull my	wrapped	crawled	building	my feet	
heart	itself	inside.	wall	coming up	

Outside   in   the   trees

a yellow bird sings green, pink lizards smile huge azure teeth,

silken scarves wrap blue feet.

I'm going to ride out of here on a white tiger.

I'm just waiting for him to

come.

What Living Means to Every Creature

No matter how different the many thousands of plants and animals may be, there are four things that every one of them must do to keep life going. They must be able to respond, to obtain and use food, to grow, and to create new beings like themselves. It is these simple actions that are the very meaning of life.

The single-cell ameba can do all these things without any limbs, nervous system, or any kind of specialized organs of digestion and reproduction. It is just a hunk of jellylike protoplasm with a nucleus. It has no fixed shape. It lives in ponds and ditches, and when the world is dry and barren, it wraps itself in a protective coating until water returns. Often it lives in the bodies of humans, sometimes causing serious diseases.

When the ameba moves, it squeezes its jellylike substance into many different shapes so that various parts called pseudopodia, or "false feet," may jut out in different directions. Just as there are reasons we sometimes walk or run, so are there reasons the ameba moves in different ways at different times. If we prod a false foot with a needle as it moves forward, the ameba may change its direction. Or it may stop altogether. Or it may pull the foot back in and push out another one in an opposite path, changing course completely. It is obvious that even though it has no nervous system, it is almost certainly capable of some sort of feeling.

The growth of the ameba is not just about getting bigger. Like other living things, it grows only because it can turn food substances into a very part of itself. As the ameba grows, so does its nucleus. This change often foreshadows an inevitable and irreversible separation.

Abridged from *Life and Its Marvels: Plant, Animal, Human.*

Dead Man

My sister insists our father have underwear on at the funeral underneath the suit we have picked out for him to be shown in. We try to tell her it doesn't matter about the underwear, he isn't going to be needing it—but it isn't a matter of reason. "Please," she says, "I just need him to have them. Will someone take a pair to the funeral home?" I tell her yes, that if she will get the pair she wants him to have, I will take them to the funeral home, which is only down at the end of the street. (Can you believe that, having a funeral home at the end of the street? I wonder if any of the houses around here have chutes in them so people can just slide the dead one along to the funeral home instead of going through all the fuss in the car, all the lights, all the neighbors poking around like they want to help but really what they want is to know it's you and not them.)

I get into my mother's gray Taurus, with my father's green bikini underwear in a brown paper bag—I am grateful that my sister didn't just expect me to hold it in the wind between my fingers like you pick up something you're not sure where it's been. Still, I am going to have to tell the tall man in the gray suit and blue tie what the heck I am doing back again, and here you go, could you please put this on my father?

When I pull open the heavy wooden door and jump through, the same man comes right over to me with his hands behind his back. I hold up the bag and start to tell him the news, but he just smiles at me like we are old friends, takes the bag, and says, "I'll take care of it." And I don't even know how he knew, but I turn and fumble out the front door and into the sunshine of the second full

day

      my

          father

             is

                dead.

sad-Lost-Sick Man

my dad is crying and it is the first time i have ever seen that;
his eyes are red, and he keeps pulling on his nose like he
is trying to make it longer. he tells me that he is very sad
because his mother died and he knows he is going to miss
her very much. his brown, wavy hair is far down on his head
like he has rubbed it with his hand many times. he looks like
a little boy, just my age, and for a moment i feel older—
maybe i can be his mother for just a minute and make him
feel better, the way mothers are supposed to do. so i put
my hand on his head and feel his little curls pop up between
my fingers kind of like grass does when you sit on it after
it's been mowed, and he just cries more like a faucet.

Sometimes at night I would find him sitting in the kitchen
having some Oreo cookies and milk before sleep. He'd be sitting
with his hands folded together like he had just done here is the
church, here is the steeple, open the door, and see all the people—
with his hands all clenched like that except now when he opened
up the church and looked inside, it was empty. He gave that feeling like when someone is playing the scales on a piano and plays
do re mi fa so la ti and then plays again *do re me fa so la ti* and again,
over and over, until it is making everyone else so crazy that someone rushes in from the other room and hits that *do* key three or
four times because they can't stand the feeling of not being able to
get on with whatever they are doing until they hear that final note.
That's how my father was; he was always looking for *do* so he
could be a full scale, and other people were always trying to show
him where it was. I always felt like I wanted to yank him down
into himself, to reach up over his head and pull down the self that
I knew was spacing out up there, looking for somewhere to go.

My father was never the kind I would see on the American Express commercials, the one who gives the kid going off to college a credit card in case she runs into problems. That dad had a real-dad look to him, with the glasses hanging down his nose and a little too much belly, and the big good-bye hug that lets the audience know that, no matter what, he's there for her. It was more backwards for me. I think my father wanted to be a real dad, but it always seemed like he might possibly need to be rescued himself, like he was always on the verge of sinking. He could never throw me a life preserver because he was too busy waiting for someone to throw his.

Maybe it was because he was so thin and he seemed to spend most of his time trying not to slip through a space in the air and be gone, just like that. Or maybe it was because his skin sagged down from his chest like an old rooster's neck and never seemed to fit him right. He had old people's skin from the very beginning, so I guess I thought my dad was always old, right from the start; I imagined him scrunching out of his mother's belly like an old prune that just kept getting older and browner, never firm and smooth. Sometimes he looked like frosting does on a cake before it gets smoothed out with a knife. He needed to have his skin moved around, tightened up—maybe secured around his back with a safety pin or tied tight like an apron. It seemed that the skin on his chest sagged the most; maybe his heart had too much sorrow in it and pulled his body down in trying to deal with all the sadness it felt.

He just got more and more into his own little world. He had always been a bit separate, so when he started to get sick, or sick as we look back on the memories, it was really hard to notice. He might have been sick for a year or so, but I'm not sure if we could tell. Even he might not have known he was sick, he had become so quiet in himself. If he forgot something, maybe he just told himself that he hadn't heard it, and if he hadn't heard it, well, he couldn't forget what he didn't know. Maybe that's how we felt, too, that his not remembering was just his not hearing. Things on the outside looked pretty much the same for a while, but there was definitely stuff on the inside coming apart, as if he were a big, old TV and someone started to pull out the wires one by one. Some of them could be pulled out and nothing would happen, but eventually the picture tube would get hit and the whole thing would blow apart.

I think that sometimes my dad wanted to grab the whole world by the collar and tell it to bug off. He seemed so angry underneath, like he could open his mouth and yell for seven years and not stop, like he wanted to throw up, all over everything. Sometimes when I looked at him, the outline of him, I would see the outline of something else barely visible, like when you stand on the edge of a dock and want to jump in, but you don't really, and you are a jumper and a nonjumper in the same place. My dad had a screamer and a nonscreamer inside, always fighting.

One time I remember him standing at the window in the living room, looking out over the backyard. A huge palm tree grew there; it was always green and had leaves so big it seemed that you could live under them and be protected. He was just standing there, staring, and suddenly he started to describe a tall evergreen tree that he said was disappearing as it was filling with snow. He was looking through a window in his mind, because as a kid he had had an evergreen tree outside his window. It was as if he had pulled down a shade on the present and was living in a room of the past. He described how the branches looked like arms being weighted down with the snow and how, when the storm was over, the tree didn't seem to be there anymore.

He became a man-child, a little kid who didn't belong in a room full of adults. He'd ask questions that weren't right for a man his age. Sometimes he would sit and talk about the old days, about his parents and the things that had happened when he really was the young age he was acting now. He could have the clearest memory of the way things were and then forget the toast he had put in the toaster a minute ago.

The staff at the nursing home would tell us that the man sitting there in the chair was no longer our father or husband but a man with a disease, and that we had to learn to separate the two. That it was the disease that said things backwards and upside down. That it was the disease that didn't recognize us or that called us a name we'd never heard of or that sometimes looked as if it might even hurt us. They said that if we could look beyond the screen the disease put up, we would see into the man who was leaving us. They said that he was still in there somewhere. If we looked really hard, we'd still see moments of him, flashes of the Bob Smith we could remember—but it wasn't something the mind could easily do. When I looked at him, I saw my father, a man struggling with a monster none of us could see. At least if I could have seen it, too, maybe then I could have helped him kill it.

When we would leave him at the nursing home, he'd start to get up out of his seat, the beginning of a stand, but we'd put our hand on his shoulder and lower him back into the chair. He'd look at us all shocked and surprised as though we had whacked him or were going to. "Please, let me come home with you," he would say.

Voices

The dog paces the room, back and forth between curtains and bed, sniffing, looking, moaning, then halts at the door, pawing to get out. A long, low moan comes from his throat, a deep rumble that grows into a howl and cuts the dark night like a siren.

"Jason," he whispers, so as not to disturb his wife. "Come."

He holds a thumb to his mouth, watching the dog's ears lean forward. Somewhere a phone rings.

"Bob, she's . . . gone."

Marion

"About an hour ago."

Marion?

"Here, Bob. I'm on the ceiling"

Marion?

"Come"

Where are you?

"Let go, Bob"

Judy, wake up, it's Marion.

"She's gone, Bob."

Judith Mary!

"You are dying, Bob"

I've got to go to work.

"Shush, you'll wake the children."

I tried to come see you

"You're too sick, Bob."

The dog, I must take the dog for a walk.

"He'll walk you to the edge"

Marion, there you are, I see you!

"I'm here, Bob"

You still have red hair

"I'll help you through"

A huge heave and wretched sobbing, then silence as the morning dawns, a single ray of light breaking through the window shade.

Lunch Break

"It's a blessing,"
they urged at church,
shook my hand
tapped my back
like I needed to burp

then invited me
to lunch,
never said another
word.

Just circled around
deviled eggs
and turkey things
like crazed ravens
stabbing
plastic knives
forks
spoons
that looked like slices
of moon
into the white
emptiness
of potato salad,
tires of orange Jell-O
rolling the table,
vacant eyes of olives
staring from
the black hutch.

They talked,
full pieces of food
hanging out,
lettuce leaves
plastered to cheeks,
legs of chickens
half devoured
rolling between their teeth.

As if death could happen
between mouthfuls,
they continued to eat.

I leaned over
picked up a tube of rolled beef
pushed my tongue
through the hole in the center
and tasted only the salt

                     of my own grief.

Part Three

The Gift

The building is one of those same buildings that line the highways of Florida. Pinkish-gray cement, orange tile roof, curved pieces lapping over and over like fake waves. In the distance, huge clouds threaten another sudden thunderstorm, that quick flash of rain that means nothing but more heat.

Mom pulls into the parking lot and guides the Ford Taurus between two yellow lines. She turns the key, flicks the set with her wrist, and sighs so completely her chest seems almost stuck in the middle of exhale, the sucking in too much to bear, the blowing out impossible to let go. "He's different," she says to me, cleaning the tip of her fingernail with the car key. "You may not see him anymore. You know, the him we know as Dad."

"How different?" I ask. "Can't be that much, I just saw him a little while ago."

"Just be ready."

My used-to-be-father is standing at the window when we arrive, dressed in madras pants that are too short and a yellow sweater that droops like a hundred kids once hung on the back of it. The sweater's sleeves are rolled up past his wrists, the right sleeve higher than the left so that he looks lopsided when he turns towards us. I slide my Ray Bans over my eyes for protection.

"Why does he have those on?" I ask. "He looks idiotic, like a clown. Aren't there some rules about how he should dress?" Mom doesn't respond, just plunks her beige knitting bag on the bed, smoothes the spread with two small strokes, and moves to him quickly. I edge into the room as if walking through fog.

"Hi, Dad," I say, lowering my shades and lipping his cheek with a quick kiss. I notice that his ears need cleaning, that his hair is bushy and crushed. His neck is fleshy and hangs as if letting go; it wobbles about like an ostrich.

The room smells litter-boxy. The walls are the color of the discarded slices of cantaloupe that sit on the breakfast trays in the hall. On the far side, framed by two windows, is a picture of three men leaning against a building in Italy or someplace where buildings are right on the water. The men are pointing at a young man who is straining to raise or lower the sail on a small boat, angling the sail up like a small compass measuring the sky. The sail seems to be luffing hard, as if it will come about in such a hurry that he might fall off the boat. In the distance, sun filters through a gray cloud, sprays rays across the blue water. Pushed up against the wall directly opposite the painting is another empty bed.

Dad doesn't speak for a minute, then tilts, almost bows in my direction. "You," he points in accusation. His finger circles the air like he's winding a piece of string. I fake a cough and turn away. Mom takes him back towards the window.

"Yes, dear, Cathy has come to visit you. Isn't that nice?"

I slide into the brown vinyl chair next to the bed, glaring at this man who is fiddling with the buttons on his shirt. I can't help staring at the wax that looks like dark dough in his ears. I want to clean them with a Q-Tip. "So," I say. Suddenly he stands up very straight, as if someone punched him in the back and told him, go ahead, get in there, the way parents push their children into the dark rooms of school. He puffs his chest huge and spreads his arms like tree branches. "Dad?" I move back in the chair, pull away.

He points at the window. "Can we go?" he pleads. "Out."

Mom nods her head vigorously, so I step into the hall and am almost run over by a small, gray woman skipping to my lou my darling down the weaving pattern of blue flox in the wall-to-wall carpet. "Oh, sorry," I say, steering around her tiny body with a fancy two-step.

The nurses station glows like a diner at the end of a long night. Two women dressed in neon-white uniforms zoomazoom from one end of the gray horizon to the other, answering phones, flipping charts, tipping little white bottles into small paper cups. A couple of slow doctors step up to the counter with stethoscopes hanging like snakes around their necks, click-clicking Bic pens in expectation.

A really, really large, nurse-Amazon woman with a red glove on her left hand looks up with big question-mark eyes. "Is it okay if I take him outside?" I ask.

"Him who?" she hmmms through beautiful teeth.

"My dad, Mr. BobRobert . . . Mr. Smith, in the room there, at the end of the hall."

She pulls her eyebrows and forehead together in a big squint that seems to help her think. "You mean the new guy, Alzheimer's? Let me check the chart," flip, flip, lick, lick pages and, "Here it is, yes, he can go out with family members. Are you?"

"I'm his daughter, and my mother's coming, too. . . ."

"Fine," she waves a ringed-out hand at me.

"There isn't a beach near here, is there? That would be nice. . . ."

"No, no, not even close. You'd have to go to the coast. To the ocean. Only water is that stream out front. You could take his shoes off and do some splashing. He might like that, you know. Little things, kind of goofy . . ." She leans to pick up a ringing phone, "Four West, Tania speaking," and I give her a thumbs-up thank you and leave.

Back in the room, Mom and Dad are sitting opposite each other with his little tray table between them as if about to play a game. "The nurse says it's okay to take him out."

"Dear, why don't you let Cathy take you for a walk. Wouldn't that be nice?"

I don't wait for him to answer, just take his arm and lead him out the door. We shuffle into the elevator, where a small green man jingles his keys like a threat and kicks the door closed with steel-tipped boots. In the foyer, someone has tucked a little army figure in one of the plastic plants that line the walls. Outside, a lemon sun drips humidity over the day, and I am choking to catch my breath.

We walk slowly past the nursing-home sign. A bird has built its nest in the O. Dad picks his leg up, bent at the knee as if broken, and pushes it forward awkwardly, like a moose. I put my hand on his shirt, feel the bumpy road of his spine going up and down.

The sky is that endless blue that only happens in Florida, that I-think-I-am-going-to-get-sick-if-I-see-another-nice-day-can't-it-just-rain-so-I-can-read-a-book-inside blue.

We say nothing. Everything seems sticky and glued. Overhead, the faint haze of a moon waits patiently. Suddenly, he stops, starts to pick at the air, moves his hands as if they are dancing.

"We shouldn't have invaded that country," he says. "I didn't say it was okay. The people were too yellow." He notices pieces of flowers in the blacktop, stoops to get them, but his fingers won't move, seem frozen. He pulls back up, turns his head, then licks his lips as if tasting the words first. "Are you going? How can you get home?"

The sky is so blue behind him, and the light from the sun shoots stars everywhere, silhouetting him. "You know," he says, "God told me this when I went to see him. That I was chosen." His head, now completely dark against the sky, takes the looming shape of a sunflower. I stop walking. He leans at me. "The sickness is a gift," he drivels, then pitches ahead into the day's raw sting.

I follow, looking up at him, realizing he is still the longest thing.

giant

it's like growing up with the empire state building, except
no elevator or gift shop, just arms, legs, feet. hands. body.
knees. dragged out bones. ankles. the rest always up there
out of sight, sticking through the clouds like some airport
tower flying the planes, talking to god on a regular basis.

in the home movies we have about our life, there is a part with
me being pushed along by a giant arm and cared for by a leg
with gray flannel pants on it. the arm keeps trying to direct
me up the brick steps to the front of the house. i want to go
around it, loop out the back, and fly away, but the arm is very
persistent and keeps guiding me home. we had some steep
steps at 29 (one of our houses, we just called them by number).
in the movie i have on my red snowsuit that had a hood with
doughy fur sticking out of it. the suit would always get zipped
right into my chin so that after a while i had a little bruise there.
my mom and dad are standing outside the house and i am
trying to hurl myself up the stairs, three steps at once, like i'm
an airplane-child that wants to come in for a landing on the top
step. it's like i don't have time to walk all the way up, i just want
to be there. each time, i am not really getting anywhere, until
my dad comes along. his body and hand reach out and give me
little pushes forward, kind of burping-moving me, even though
i am well past being burped at that point.

in another movie i am playing softball with a giant hand.
over and over the hand shovels the ball to me, and i swing
and swing and swing. then i curl down and toss it back in
a big circle over my head. the hand reaches in and grabs it

before it falls to the ground, as if saving it from something. i never hit it; it just goes flying right by my ear and into the bushes. but i never give up trying, and the ball just keeps coming at me. i know my dad is the one throwing the ball; even though i can't see him, i can see him.

living with a giant does have its advantages. no matter how high something is put away, he can always reach it for you. we have a huge christmas tree because he can reach the top without having to drag out the ladder and clamber about. he even puts lots of colored lights with foil pretties around them all the way up, not petering out like the trees where someone can't reach that high and just throws an angel up there.

giants are also really good at saving the day. when a neighbor's washing machine is on the blink and starts doing a dance around the kitchen, it is my dad who is called to man the lifeboat. he goes running down the street with two floppy mops over his shoulders, looking like a giant soldier. my mother goes down a little later to supervise the whole matter, but by then dad has things completely under control. he stands on feet wet to the ankles in the middle of a shining sea, slapping the mop around with those big shoulders that always seem to be taking orders—shoulder one to shoulder two, come in shoulder two—like twins with walkie-talkies or something. the neighbor has fixed him up with a couple of drippy drinks, so he hurries to get to those.

he has a tiny car, dark blue with a flag on the back. he loves that car with all of his might and when he pulls into the driveway at night, hair all blown at his face and a wild, gold grin a mile long, he is the biggest thing around in the smallest thing possible. it looks like he has been lowered by a crane into the seat. how else can he get in there, with those bony legs and ankles and shoes, trying to fit underneath that shiny wooden wheel? how do you fold up a giant?

he is always bending into or out of other people's lives, leaning down if he wants to be with you. you have to carry a ladder with you if you want to be in his world all the time. at parties, his hands disappear into the ceiling when he dances, which he almost always does. he dances as if he's in some tribal country where there are no lights or machines. or maybe in that world up above his shoulders, he hears different music than we hear down here on earth. anyway, he holds his hands way up above his head and shakes them like rattles, maybe praying to the sky for rain or some other kind of help. he shakes and shakes, throws his head back out over his neck, and gives a huge clap as if he has finally figured something out. then he leans way back and sort of bounces in place like he has found an invisible bench to sit on. he stays that way sometimes even after the music and voices have stopped.

he talks to you about anything you feel like bringing up, but you have to be real careful if you ask him a question. if there is a hurry involved, better not to ask because he will give you the longest answer possible, with every detail and some you would never think to ask. if you have any plans with friends, forget it. his answers are like those roads way out west where you never seem to get anywhere. i think he just likes to have someone to listen to him, or maybe he just wants someone to look at him for a long time.

mostly he talks about gigantic ships that sink in the night or
ram into each other. he talks about the andrea doria and how
the bow crashes into another boat and scoops a little girl
right out of her sleeping bunk and drops her almost onto the
anchor of another ship, and how they find her there on the
bow many hours later still okay, not drowned, just amazed.
sometimes he talks as if he is the captain of the ship and
describes everything about the boat as if he sees it in another
life. he tells what the ship does so that it won't sink, and you
think if only they had called dad, things would be different
and lots of dead people would still be around. probably dad
could just reach in and pop the people back on the boat,
shake them off, and give them a towel. the titanic is his
favorite story. every time he talks about the ship, it sinks even
deeper. he says they hit an iceberg, and icebergs have a lot
more underneath than is up on top, and no one who was
steering the boat knew that, but they should have. i think,
what are they doing driving around icebergs anyway? how
about just a straight path of ocean so no one gets hurt? he
says they tried to get people off, but still a million of them
are left floating alone in the dark sea, and he looks down at
where his heart is like he knows them personally, his friends
or something. he says that the guy who built the boat thought
it could hit just about anything and still be okay, but that
people are usually wrong when they think that everything
is going to be okay no matter what.

a typical day in a giant's family at forest road—where we live
because a friend of dad's said, "you should move onto our
street because we have ninety children, more kids than you

can shake a stick at"—is we all get up and stuff us kids into the car. We drive my dad to the station, one, two, or three of us, however many there are depending on who stayed over at someone else's house for the night. then we come home and have breakfast with white donuts that make designs all over the place and even smell in your nose after they are gone. then mom takes us to some lady with a playgroup, and the grown-ups do wild dances and stick their chests way out and the rest of us kids play and run around. when that is enough of that we go home to have lunch on blue plastic plates that spin around after the sandwich is gone. naps are supposed to happen at this point, but we'll see about that depending on the day and who is sleepy, which is usually just mom, not us kids. we are always looking for ways to stay awake for our whole lives.

then in a couple of minutes it's time to go get dad at the station where the train wakes him up and spits him out at us, and i'm in the back seat watching this long rocket man take a sweep across the parking lot and see us with a big smile— there they are, i'm saved—and he comes on over and opens the door and i can hardly wait at all for the giant to really arrive.

when you need someone to be at the head of things, call a giant. a giant can put everything—like a family—in nice rows, making steps that lead the family to a good life. especially this is true for taking pictures. we are in a million shots looking like little stairways that anyone could walk up or down on their way to heaven. right before the picture, i press my shoes together so tight that they squeak, and i try to get them exactly even so that nobody is out in front, just at the starting line. i have on my white gloves with the little ridges in between each finger and i play with my thumb until my mom tells me stop fidgeting (even though i am not really fidgeting, just trying to hook my thumb under one of those ridges because it feels good, like it has found a home). my little sister has on a hat with plastic fruit, and the strap around her chin leaves a little red line when she takes it off. my other sister has those glasses that sparkle. we move closer together so that there is no space between us, no distraction, just a straight drop from shoulder to shoulder, and guess who is taking the picture up there at the front like the tallest flower, always at the beginning of things with his head in the clouds.

if you laid him down on the ground, you could probably measure out a whole house to build. just lay him four times in a row—feet to head, feet to head, feet to head, feet to head—and clearly you would have enough space to live a whole life in.

Women and Children First

November 25, 1962

Dear Judy,

Well, it's 9:30 Sunday evening, the children are sound asleep after a riotous evening, the diapers are sloshing around in the laundry, the bulbs are in, the storm window is back in place on Cathy's window, and we are all intact. We miss you, rather more than we expected to, I imagine—each one of us has said we miss you at one time or another—but we are still absolutely okay. We are even well fed. Not a poached egg has sullied the table, just turkey and roast beef, peas, squash, potatoes, dressing, and at lunch, peanut butter and jelly, cheese, and we've had a run on apple sauce.

The first night Cathy called me in many times to get precise details on your schedule, and particularly your return, and she said she missed you. But no tears. Today at lunch, she suddenly flew apart, burst out crying, and crawled into my lap saying she wanted you back. That was the most dramatic outburst we've had, and all the rest of the time they carry on as if nothing were unusual.

At one point yesterday little Joanie nearly broke my heart by first getting fussy—it was nearly supper time and we were raking leaves and she had had about enough of the whole deal, so she walked from the back garden through the gate to the play area and saw the car in the turn-around and said, in a small, inquiring voice, "Mommy?"

I dropped everything and went over to her and in no time she was under a pile of leaves laughing with the others. Poor little poop, she is such a good girl. She has hardly coughed at all, by the way. I don't think I've heard her cough once today.

Going to church was an epic disaster. I just didn't leave

enough time. All were fed, beds were made, we were listening to the duck record your mother gave them—we've been doing that all weekend, and I'm now fed up with what I originally thought was a charming tale. The damn duck was a fool and deserved to be stuffed with sage and onions. But anyway, we were going great. I decided to get going, got them all dressed, realized it was 10:30 and I was not dressed, so I shaved at top speed, cut myself, put on a shirt, got blood on the shirt, took it off, grabbed another one, found it was my sport shirt, threw it on the bed, grabbed another one, pulled on my clothes, pushed them all into their coats, tested the side door (I had painted it), found it okay, sent them out. Polly opened the screen door (which was not okay), turned around, and was white from stem to stern on the starboard side. So back we came, I cleaned child and coat with turpentine, and, reeking like a paint store, we set off, dramatically late, to get Cathy in just under the wire and me standing up at the back of the church. I wound up a few minutes later balancing on a tiny chair halfway down the aisle.

And we went all through the litany, which Don Back said was a custom now for the last Sunday of every month, which I say is, on the face of it, a good argument in favor of the Mormons.

I've talked only about us, on a rather mundane level, but that's the level we're on, and it's awfully cozy and nice. I hope you're having fun, because we are, despite your being away. I thank heaven for the children because they make the days warm and fun and help a lot to fill up the rather boring hole that's left when you're away.

Say hello to everyone, and tell yourself that I love you, because I do.

Bob

Dream   *My mother and I are going to visit him. He is living way out in the country in France, and we are astonished because we thought all this time that he was dead. I don't know how we came to find him in the new home, but we are elated. The trip takes us through lush forests and beautiful gardens, the train zigzagging through an amazing landscape. When we finally arrive, Dad is standing on his head and won't come down. My mother asks him what he has been doing here all this time and why did he pretend to die. He won't answer us, just stands there on his head until a long, thin man in red sneakers comes and tells us we must leave. My father still refuses to speak and we board the train in anguish and say nothing more on the ride away from him.*

FINDING SAFETY IN NUMBERS

Many animals find safety and achieve a better livelihood by living together in groups of varying size.

The simplest and smallest community is the family. Members in a family form a single, close-knit unit and often stay together even after young members are old enough to take care of themselves, as seen in the family of birds.

Among certain higher mammals, the mother watches over and feeds the young ones for months. The father carries on this protection for many years after.

Several baboon families often unite, forming a single herd under the leadership of an old male baboon. Often this male will rule in ways similar to a dictatorship, as he claims all the females as his wives.

There are advantages to living this kind of communal life. Those members of the herd that are keen listeners and seers can be posted as lookouts to warn the herd of approaching danger.

Sometimes, fairly large groups of grazing animals will allow themselves to follow a chosen leader blindly. Elephants often live in herds led by an old female. The leader most times earns her position by her vigilant watch over the members of the herd, keeping them from any outside danger. But sometimes the leader can become ill-tempered and savage, either from an accident or from an illness. In this event, the entire herd can also become dangerous and destroy anything and everything in its path.

Abridged from *Life and Its Marvels: Plant, Animal, Human.*

Heavy Hits

It happens, another shift
cracking the sky door's   giant rift.

Landscape invasion, tin-ringing
applefeet, sheets slapping   wind flapping wheat
jackspeed.

Crazy sunshift, capital
lift, parallel dive, a wicked eye   peering inside.

Then nothing.
          Then silence.
                    Then life

     splitting,

the slash of light on cattails
the marshgrass lifting.   The sigh.

Wild Kingdom

The nurse with the giraffe neck meets us at the door as we are buzzed in. "Now, it's not as bad as you think." Her hair looks like a submarine on the top of her head, tipping on the way to sinking.

My mother blows out some exhaust. "What?" she stammers, stepping forward.

The giraffe flicks her pen at us, lifts the page on a chart. "Well, he got into someone's room somehow. Everyone was asleep. She woke up. He broke her arm. Pushed her down."

Mom collapses into the brown plastic chair that shines like it's just been cleaned.

"What happened?" I ask.

"We don't really know; as I said, everyone was asleep. Sally woke up and started screaming, 'Monster, monster.' She was probably still dreaming. I guess she frightened him, and he just flipped, started hitting her, mumbling on about getting dressed for work. He's big, you know. And strong. Broke her arm." Giraffe-lady shrugs, like this kind of thing happens all the time. Pretty normal or something like that.

My father is living inside an Alzheimer's ward at a nursing home in North Carolina. No, actually, my father is locked in a ward at a nursing home in North Carolina. He actually lives elsewhere these days, places he doesn't take any of us.

I am furious. "Why wasn't anyone watching him? How did he get into her room? Don't you lock anything around here?"

We know the ward itself is locked twenty-four hours a day. "For the patients' safety," is what everyone says, so that a father or mother or sister or uncle doesn't wander away and end up on the highway going north without any identification or a way to get home or even an inch of memory left that knows where home is. The brochure mentions this over and over again: being safe, having peace of mind.

"Forget it," I say, and lean down for my mother. I take her arm, and we walk the cream-colored slate floor, past the ghosts and residents, to his room.

He is sitting in the chair, running his finger over his lower lip. "Need a shave," he smiles. My mom reaches into the room with her body all crooked and cocked sideways, as if she's both coming and leaving, and kisses his cheek.

"Hi, dear." She pats down the hair on his head and reaches for the comb on the dresser. He looks at her as if he actually knows who she is, and for a minute, it seems that he is here, back from a long trip or a very deep sleep. I go over and hold his bony hand.

"Hi, Dad."

He looks at me. "I know you," he says, winking as if from bright light. "You're from far away." The chair moves as he leans his head back to rest from the efforts of a small remember. He opens his mouth too wide, and I can see all the way past his back teeth, almost past the uvula, that punching bag in the throat. Almost to the end of him.

The giraffe comes in. "I think everything is going to be fine," she says. I don't turn around to face her, just leave her stranded behind me.

"Where are his glasses?" I ask.

"Well, let's look in his usual place." She flaps in, curves down in front of Dad, and reaches for the rubber plant on his window-sill. "Nope," she throats. "Not there . . . hmmm."

"Why are you looking in the plant?" my mother asks, in a carefully normal tone of voice so that it sounds as if she is asking about a perfectly reasonable situation when actually you could have lit a bunch of firecrackers off the tension in the room.

"Because that's where he always puts them. No matter how

hard we try to put them in his glasses case, he just puts them back in the plant." She scratches a red pimple on her neck, then starts to pick at it like she might pop it off. Maybe if she does, all the air that's holding up her neck will come out and her head will come back down to where it belongs, near her shoulders, where everybody's head should be when they are supposed to be thinking straight and helping a crazy man find his way.

It's like living in a jungle, I think.

"Hey," my father half-screams, half-says. He turns his head from side to side in deep disagreement with the situation. His eyes are turned upward like he is waiting for directions or just trying to keep the gush of tears from falling over and down the sides of his cheeks.

I turn away and start opening his dresser drawers, determined to find the glasses.

"Maybe some music," Mom says, turning on the tiny transistor radio propped on the table by the lamp. Tinny strings and trebly bass prick the air like gnats, and I flick it off quickly. Dad begins to hum.

"Forget the glasses," I say, slamming the last dresser drawer. "Let's just get him a couple of pairs so you'll always have one, Mom. If this place loses them, just pull one out of your purse. Can't we just go to the drugstore and buy some generic brand, like three pairs?" Mom nods slowly, as if the effort to do so will kill her.

Dad continues his humming, and I suddenly realize the sound is his impersonation of an electric razor. I walk out the door and down the hall to the nurses station, where the giraffe seems to have escaped into deep cover. An older woman with a wide body and weirdly pointed hair asks what she can do for me. I wonder if a miracle is in her repertoire but ask only if my father can get a shave. She nods and assures me a male attendant will be down shortly, so I turn and accidentally kick a small tabby cat figure-eighting around my legs.

"Oh, sorry, is this . . . what's a cat doing in here?"

"That's Monday, she lives here. Animal therapy cat. The residents love her, think she is the collective reincarnation of all their pets. Actually, she often sleeps on the end of your father's bed."

I go back to the room. Dad is lying down and Mom is reading one of the paperback mystery stories she keeps in her purse for helping to pass unbearable time.

"Did you find his glasses?" she asks, without looking up from her book.

"Nope, but they are going to shave him. Couple of minutes."

I watch my father sleeping on the bed, knees pulled up to his chest, a man who has never in his whole life slept in a bed that was long enough.

Dream *I find him living in Japan, and I am screaming at him, why did you leave us, how could you be here with another family? But he is not quite right, and when I reach out to touch him, pieces flake away, as if he were a fine pastry. When he turns sideways, I can see that he is flat, like a billboard, that there is really nothing there. Then the dog comes into the room, and he is flat, too, and he falls over with a loud thud; and when I look down, there is no dog, just a piece of board. Then the whole family starts speaking in Japanese and I am asked to leave, and my father doesn't move or speak, he is just frozen in place, with no dimension.*

Conversation: IV

Cathy: And then there was always the station car. Not a wagon. It was a German car

Mom: He would put on his overcoat and get in the station car and be gone. Then in reverse, he'd come home, take his coat off, and have a drink

Polly: I can still smell those plastic glasses we had on the boat. The gin or vodka just went right into the plastic

Mom: We had that big ice pick for chipping the ice for drinks. You would never let your kids near one now. We used to sink our cans and watch them disappear

Joan: We used to play pencil. Jump in the water and try to get the pencil

Mom: He was very happy when he was on that boat. Those were good times

Polly: When I think of him, it is overwhelming, him sick in the nursing home

Joan: Senior year, I had him all to myself

Polly: I can remember my wedding as if I am looking at a movie. He had Oreos in his pocket. He was afraid he would cough, so he put the Oreos in his pocket in case he coughed. They were all crumbs. He totally laughed at that. I remember what he said to me as we began walking down the aisle. He said, "Well, here we go. This is it." How did he know?

Mom: I remember very well Dad being ill, getting iller. I remember just a losing battle. Thinking how quiet things were getting

Polly: I had a lot invested in Dad. I was convinced he was going to get better. It was like a crusade. I was even going to reverse Alzheimer's. He was going to come out of it

Joan: You had the opportunity to, because we weren't there

Cathy: Yeah, Pol, you lived so close . . . too close

Polly: I just knew if I made that room pretty enough, if we bought all the pretty things and the throw and the chair and the pretty rug . . . I thought, we'll make the room okay, and he will be okay. The room looked wonderful, and he would bring other people by to look at the room. When he died, I went to the nursing home because I wanted to talk to the nurse who was with him. He was the first patient who ever died on her. "Where are his belongings?" I asked. She opened up a closet and inside there was the chair and the plastic wrap and his glasses on the top of the bag. That was all that was left. And a little nurse going by asked for the chair, and I said okay. There was something devastating about that chair being in the closet. It just minimized his existence. It wasn't even a nice closet. It was just too visual

Mom: But with Dad, he would say things that just . . . I would take him out for ice cream and take him to the McDonald's down the road and get him a sundae, and it would be such a struggle to get him into the car

Cathy: He wouldn't bend

Mom: We couldn't get him back into the car. And then Cathy came, and we went to the beach. He wouldn't get back into the car. He could understand getting into the van, because you stepped up and sat, and he could get that concept, but he couldn't get the bend. In the end, when he would get hold of your hand, he would not let go. He didn't know how to let go. He reached out and grabbed a lady's hand, and she couldn't get it back. We had to pry his fingers off

Polly: My last memory—we were outside, at a white table with an umbrella on top of it. I remember sitting there. I really didn't want to . . . it didn't cross my mind that that would be the last time I would see him

Joan: It's been a while. . . . He was always really nice to me. Even though at the end he didn't know my name, I kind of felt like he still knew me. He didn't know me, physically me, but he knew me on another level, in another world

Mom: You can never know how much an Alzheimer's patient knows. . . . They recognize something

Polly: And when he fell out of bed, broke his hip

Joan: Who got the call

Polly: I got the call from the emergency room. "Is this Polly Roth? Are you related to Robert Smith?" "Yes," I said, "I'm his daughter." And then I told them that he has Alzheimer's, and he will be really scared; he won't know who you are, and he needs to have someone hold his hand

Mom: I was at a party. It was Valentine's Day—a party. And who called you? Nobody called me. The party was over, and we took some flowers to visit him. As soon as I got there: "We have been trying to contact you," they said. They had been trying to find me since one o'clock. "I think I upset your daughter," the doctor said

Polly: I had to give my permission to save his life. He must have been scared

Joan: I think that is why you see him as ill. You were part of all this stuff. We would hear about it a week later, but we weren't directly involved. I thought of Dad's illness as just an illness. I didn't see it. To me, Dad had textbook Alzheimer's. To you, Dad had living Alzheimer's

Polly: I would hold his hands. They were so old. The skin was tight on them. I would look him in the eye and wait for the connection. I would chat about absolutely nothing. He seemed simply to like the sound of a person's voice. And, of course, the famous question I asked him

Cathy: Do you have any children

Polly: "Yes," he said. "I have three, and one turned out really fine." Of course, we all know who

Joan: I remember at the wake, when I finally got up to the casket, I had to move his finger to make sure that it moved. I had read a short story about embalming, and I needed to know that his hands were just the way they had always been, not sewn down in some strange way. I think I put a flower in his hands

Cathy: Mom and I went to get him a pair of glasses; remember, Mom? You couldn't look at him without them.

When She Saw Him

By the time she arrived at the nursing home, it had already been a full morning on the wing. One of the residents had lost her prosthesis, and there had been quite a ruckus trying to find it, pulling other residents' dressers open and searching around. It seemed she had a habit of putting it somewhere else, not on her leg where it belonged; no matter how many times they told her, she'd find a new stash for it. Maybe she did it because it made her feel that at least she could make a decision about where something was to be put, since she was probably left out of the decision to be placed here, the worst decision a family ever has to make.

So things were kind of chaotic, which was nothing new for an Alzheimer's ward, and everyone was bouncing off the walls and talking like train wrecks and she could see that the nurses had their hands full, but she couldn't imagine how full.

Whenever she walked down the long hall, she tried not to look into the residents' rooms, because she couldn't stand it, didn't want to see the looks and stares, the hands reaching towards the door in pathetic anticipation. She thought, please just don't look back at me I can't help you I've got a father here who is dying too and I can only deal with one thing at a time you'll have to call your own family I'm already booked.

Even the look into her father's room can twist her up in a single second so that the rest of the visit she's just trying not to let out a wail so loud it would seem to be coming from the beginning of time. Because he would always be sitting there, in that chair that looked like it belonged in a normal person's living room, with his hair all Albert-Einsteined and wild, maybe a bit of drool on his chin dropping to the knuckle on his hand. Or he'd be sleeping, head crooked to the side as if his neck were broken, like someone had turned his head and tried to snap it off, or maybe they had tried to empty out his brain and put in a new one, thank God, but forgot to screw his head back on tight.

So today, when she takes the deep breath down to her toes before she swings her body in front of the door frame, she chokes on an arrow of air when she doesn't see him at all, because, of course, she thinks, that's it, why didn't they tell us it had happened, how could they let me come and find out by myself. I can't believe he has died and no one told us. Where is my dead father?

But then a little squirt of noise in the corner makes her look, and she sees Howard, his minister-roommate, holding her dad in his arms, a little pudgy man cradling a huge tree of a man as if about to baptize him, lower him into the river.

Nurse

The nurse sits down at her kitchen table and opens a bottle of Diet Coke, feeling a sense of relief as the *pffffssttt* fills the air around her. She takes a swig, plops the bottle back on the table, and reaches for a bag of pretzels, which she opens loudly and with vigor. Her hand grabs six at once, setting them down on the table in front of her, little hearts of carbs and salt. Lord have mercy will she ever lose some weight?

Outside, the wind slashes against the window as if about to enter. Rainstorms in Florida can be violent in their suddenness, in their unrelenting energy and force. Just forty minutes ago the sun was shining as she stepped out of the nursing home, marking the end of the day she lost her first patient.

The soda sizzles softy in the glass, tickles her nose like an invisible feather; she takes another gulp.

She knew him as a quiet, gentle man who seemed to be waiting for death to slip around the corner and take him. It was as if he had accepted the end and let go. Over coffee one morning, the other nurses told her about his violent episodes, the seething when he came in, picking up furniture with the intent of smashing the living daylights out of anybody in his way, grabbing visitors and staff in an iron-vice grip, screaming all day like a banshee. They said he had to be restrained, attached to the furniture like a packing slip.

She had found all this hard to believe. Each morning when she arrived at work, she would check on him, nudge the shade open so as not to wake him; though he was always awake. He would almost smile at her, or maybe it was at someone behind her, she thought now. His face had no anger, no rage—it was almost completely blank, as if everything had been poured away.

"Good morning, Mr. Smith," she would say. "How did you sleep?"

He didn't speak anymore. Actually, she had never heard him say anything. "Since the accident," the nurses whispered.

It had happened two days before she came. He'd fallen out of bed, or so the nurses thought since no one seemed to know, just assumed that that must have been how he broke his hip. The amazing thing was, Mr. Smith had managed by morning to get back into bed on his own, broken hip and all, even pull the sheet back up to his chin.

However, when breakfast arrived, he didn't eat. He didn't move, didn't rise from the bed. Then lunch, dinner, and by early evening, he was gawking and reeling in pain. At first, everyone thought it was just the torment of his disease, a flooding rampage getting ready to burst through the dam and slam anything in its way. They began to brace themselves, prepared to restrain him, tie him to the bed. One attendant lifted the sheet, jerked it out from underneath him, and when Mr. Smith fainted, saw the swelled hip all black and bruised.

The soda gone, she pushes her chair back and goes to the front door, which she opens slowly. The rain is letting up, so she decides to keep it open, get some air, even though the foyer tiles are wet and slippery. She leans out the screen door and looks up at the sky.

The night nurse told her they had to search for the wife, finally had to call his daughter in North Carolina, listed as next of kin, for permission to operate, which she gave through desperate pleas to please, someone, hold his hand, he will be scared. The ambulance attendant said Mr. Smith cried for his mother the whole ride there.

When she herself had arrived at the home, another job in a long slew of them, she had decided to really make a go of it, stay in one place, take things seriously. And even when it got hard, which she knew it would, to stick her chin out, dig her feet in, and hold on with the strength Jesus would give her Amen if she could just believe in his glory.

For the next three weeks, she believed God would heal this man, allow him to walk again, take his twisted brain, sieve out the disease, and show him the way of the Lord. She prayed for him at night, prayed he would sit up and speak, prayed she could be a channel through which Jesus would work his blessings. She believed this even as he stopped eating completely, when he stopped looking, when the bedsores bled profusely as she tried to turn his bony, graceless body with a tenderness that was not hers. She smiled at him always, at his wife who sat next to the bed and knit long swatches of pain, at the lawyer who came to help with the decision to insert a feeding tube.

So this morning, when she slipped into his room and found him sitting up, pillows propped behind his head—something he must have done himself—she knew the Lord Almighty had done His work.

"Why, Mr. Smith, my goodness, look at you!"

He gave a small wave with an emaciated hand, then made a motion, which at first seemed to be uncontrolled shaking, until she realized he was telling her he wanted something to eat.

"Are you hungry?" she asked, and he nodded.

"Well, Glory Hallelujah, Amen, thank you, Lord."

The rain is letting up, and the day looks like it's just been through the car wash, all squeegeed clean and polished. She thinks about taking a walk down by the pond, maybe feed the ducks, sit on the bench and breathe, and she goes to her room to rummage for the new sneakers she bought last week.

So this morning, when the lawyer was scheduled to return with the papers for the wife to sign, Mr. Smith ate the biggest breakfast possible, as if he were making up for all the weeks he had been starving. She had to help him a bit, but he managed to do

163

most of the work himself, raising and lowering the fork gently and without pause. He gulped his milk in three swallows, held the glass out for more, then took the second one slowly, as he must have been full, but wanted to store up for an unexpected trip on which he might expend all his energy. He tipped his head way back, let the last bit trickle down his chin, and placed the glass carefully back on his tray.

"Let me get that little bit," she'd said, dabbing with a napkin.

The gasping started immediately. She thought it might be food stuck in his throat, so she ran behind and slapped him on his back. "Mr. Smith, Mr. Smith!" He began to slide down the pillows as if he were liquid, a smooth movement towards the bed, a final all-in-one motion as if rehearsed, a perfect movement of athletic grace. She raced for her supervisor, who hurried back with her into the room.

"It's happening," she said. "I'll call his wife."

"Mr. Smith, can you hear me? Mr. Smith, it's me, Mary."

He opened his eyes when he heard that, started to reach as if to touch her face, as if to take it with him. She grabbed his hand and held it.

"Mr. Smith, I'm here. I'm right here. Hold on. Your wife is coming. Jesus, hold on."

With that, he exhaled himself into death ten minutes before his wife arrived, riding the cusp of a giant wind that would carry him forward to meet the Lord.

Which is what she said to the wife. "The Lord took him peacefully. I held his hand."

funny man

one night when mom is home, we are all sitting down to
dinner in the usual way, everyone in their assigned places,
though not like anyone says you sit here, you sit here, or
uses any nametags or anything, just everyone knows their
chairs. it is a quiet day, not dressing up for work or running
around to meetings and clubs and dinner parties, just all the
family hanging around the house, standing around with some
smiles and wishing. dad lumbers up to the table with his
favorite shirt on, the one with the blue and red stripes, the
shirt he wears when he isn't planning any work in the yard,
just a shirt for shirt's sake, and he sits down and begins
to cut up the meat and drop it onto everyone's plate. roast
beef, my favorite. i am watching, hoping to grab a little piece
before i get my real helping, so i am leaning forward towards
the meat plate and for some reason, i move my head to look
at his shirt. would you believe it, on his shirt, instead of the
stripes that we think we see—you know, like a regular shirt
will have stripes on it—there are actually a million little mickey
mouses, all hanging on to each other like they are jumping
out of an airplane and floating down with invisible capes on
my daddy's shirt. mickey mouse and the whole gang right
there in the dining room. dad can't believe it, so off comes
the shirt. he gets his glasses, and sure enough, there they
are. he thinks it is hilarious, and from that day on i never
see the stripes again, just mickey, and i can't believe he
was there all the time and no one knew.

The Man Who Died Long Ago

When he did die, on March 20, 1991, at 8:10 in the morning, and the phone call came to my office—my sister crying on the other end, trying to give the details with the reassurance that he was free now—I felt the odd sensation that I was hearing news I'd already known. A part of me wanted to respond, yes, I know he's dead; you are years late with the news. Of course, I felt the immediate tear, the ripping away and straight pain to the heart, the arrow across the sun and stunned realization that it was finally over. But he'd been dead for years already, his whole being leaking away, leaving an empty vessel that moved through the halls of the nursing home like an abandoned ship, its crew long dead and nearly forgotten.

I'd actually practiced hearing the news, many times, and how I could react. On my evening walks, I'd imagine the phone call coming, and where I would be, and how I would look and move and tip my head forward with grief or lean back in my chair breathing a sigh of relief. How does one really understand the death of a parent? More difficult, how do you grasp the death over and over, all the small ones that precede the final hour? Every time I saw him, he had died some more, as if pieces of him were falling away.

So when I actually heard that all of him had died, I heard the echo of death through the room like a fading heartbeat, and I knew I'd been here many times before.

HONING IN

Some insects seem able to distinguish clearly between different colors. The Vanessa butterfly, for instance, has a marked preference for red, and almost always seeks out red flowers.

Abridged from *Life and Its Marvels: Plant, Animal, Human.*

Dream   *I am sleeping and suddenly a comet splits through the ceiling and into the room. Light explodes a new vision: animals in the distance, at the park, seem touchable. Giraffe, zebra dance under the trees, flip upside down like acrobats. Fish swim underneath the bed of glass, their huge eyes staring blue and yellow, irises wide and alive. On the far wall, flashes of life appear like a kaleidoscope, colors and diamonds and circles. We are standing in a row, he is leading us, he is leaning with my mother on the bridge, his long arm around her shoulder and the water and the waves. We are singing at the table, saying grace, he is laughing, he is climbing through thick leaves, and I see him, handing down a lost cat. Then I don't see him. Then the parking lot, and I see him loping away, away from the nursing home and into the night.*

The First Time Dead

We are in the private viewing room. Our name, Smith, is on a little sign at the top of the door. Like royalty or something. It is a room at the end of a hall, actually one of two rooms, one on either side of a carpeted and silent darkness. We had all looked around before entering, as if we weren't sure this was the right place, though we knew perfectly well that, of course, this was the place; what else could it be?

The door had been open, which was good because we needed that to get ourselves in. If the door had been closed, we might just have thought, that's the end of that, and turned around, you know how you want to do when you know that something really big could just knock the wind out of your sails and turtle you down into the dark ocean. So we just walked in, like we might arrive at a party, except it was completely still, as if everyone had stopped breathing when we got there, just like the man in the coffin at the other end of the room. Of course, we all knew this man, knew perfectly well it was our father, except I think we all hoped there might be some mistake.

This will be the first time I have seen him dead, even though I have looked at that possibility in my mind for several days. I don't really know what a dead father will look like, or how to act around one. A friend told me to never touch a dead body, because then you have dead on you and you can't wipe it off, but I have to make sure this is the real thing. I begin moving towards him. My sisters come with me, followed by my mother, who is making strange little sounds.

"He doesn't look real," I say, "more like he's plastic. Do you think it's really him? Maybe it just looks like him. A statue." By now we are even with the coffin. We stop. I reach in and fumble with a button on his shirt. My sister gasps.

173

"Don't do that," she says fiercely, pushing my hand away. "For God's sake."

"What, I just want to feel his skin. I want to see if it's him."

"Of course it's him," she says. "What do you think . . ."

But I want to know, so I open his shirt and put my hand in, move it around, feel how smooth it is, waxy, like mannequin skin, but thin, as if I might erase it with too much pressure.

I feel his face, touch his forehead. It's cold. His cheeks are shiny, almost glistening, but no sweat. Hair combed on the wrong side. Lips parted. No words, no breath. Nothing.

He is the biggest thing I've ever seen dead like this. Completely dead all the way through, not just hit by a car and still dying some.

I wonder how they get someone this big and dead into the coffin, how they stuff him in there. Is there a crane or machine, because he must weigh a thousand pounds, like a mountain or a boulder or something that people don't normally have to pick up. Aren't you heavier when you're dead?

So I'm thinking about this huge thing here all packed into white clouds and frilly lace, which my father would never in real life have let himself lean on, and I realize that even though he is dead and there is nothing we can do about it and that no matter what, those eyes are going to stay sewn shut, there is also something good here, a loud silence around him, as if everything in the room has its finger to its lips, shushing something up.

And then I know what it is. I know it's gone.

"He isn't sick anymore," I say. "Look at his face. It's clear. Quiet. He's almost smiling."

My sister Joan takes a daisy out of the flowers we had ordered (no gladiolas, my mother had told us, they are just funeral flowers) and puts it on his chest. Then we all step back, and we can leave now because we know he's off somewhere, flying about on his way up to God, this huge burst of our father who was finally let out.

We turn to leave, and we walk through the still funeral home where people don't say anything to us, just nod and tight-lip it, and we all say nothing, just put our hands by our sides to take the weight off. We reach the big front door and one of the quiet people hands us our coats and pushes open the door into a yellow flood of sunshine where we stand for a minute and watch a huge butterfly slide right out of the air and head for Mom, for the red flower she has on her dress.

the missing link

one night after dinner, dad says, "your father is a very
unusual man," as if this is news to us. we are all sitting out
on the patio he had made by hand, brick by brick. it was a
huge job, lugging all that stuff around from the side of the
house, and he had sweated a whole river down his back
doing it and hadn't minded at all.

"when i was a little boy," he says, "i had a tusk growing right
out of my mouth, straight out like a rhinoceros, and," he says,
flapping his hand behind him, "i also had a tail." i try to picture
him as an animal let loose somewhere in the jungle with this
wild tooth leading the way.

"people used to say i was a missing link," he says.

"what's a missing link?" my sister asks.

"well, it's sort of a new species all its own, a bridge—
half man, half creature."

"what happened to the tail?" a couple of us ask. "do you
still have it?"

"no," he says, "the doctors took it out so i could sit down.
they made me just a normal man, like everyone else." then
he plops himself onto the patio wall and crosses his legs.

i try to picture a missing link, and all i see is a hairy shadow
walking on very straight legs, tipping from side to side, a big
lug of a thing pushing its way into places it doesn't belong,
scaring the daylights out of children and dogs.

Disease-Man

I have no children.

Friday, June 23, 1986

Dear Cathy,

Now there is a hat. I never had a hat. It's great. Certainly on the beach and also anywhere—even in the shade—because it's very smart looking. I just feel good in it. Thank you. It feels good to have it on. And it makes sun very safe. What a neat way to celebrate getting a year older.

Dad

I have no children.

Saturday, June 24, 1986

Dear Joanie,

That's a terrific picture of sailboats in an industrial harbor. I raced a bit for a while, and the boats anchored in New Haven looked just like that. Thank you for a clear and exciting memory.

Dad

I have no children.

Sunday, June 25, 1986

Dear Polly,

You certainly know where I am happy: in the presence of a gaff-rigged sloop. You gave me one with dazzling blue sails, and she is on top of the TV. I find I often ignore the TV and stare at that great ship model from you. The hell with TV. First things first. Thank you for a wonderful gift, Polly.

Dad

The Glory Walk

1.

Winter panic again
gray days fisting low desires
wheat fields yellow with rain.
Across the rows silver skycrows
trap blue heights and pathways higher,
circle back and back again.

2.

Stumbling across the horizon
sights of lost life:
a childdog climbing down
from the grave,
glued glaze of a parent's eye—
a lover's distant blade.

3.

Then memory, that unbearable
leech, cleaves to the bone,
pushing the soul
like an abandoned swing,
a shack-strapped
and shining thing.

4.

I know there are points in my life
when someone could have saved me,

taken up the shame in her soft white hand
like a clay wing,
pulled it into something I could carry
to the water
and edge away on.

5.

Overhead black holes hand
a white skeleton down,
cloud patient dazed
in the last stage of grief.
A sad bird urges
the moon to emerge
in full sun
like a desperate thief.

6.

If only we were told
the number of days
we hold in our hand,
life's limits would be
a white kiss in the sky,
blaze of light like a fire rod
torching the tip of the heart—

setting up the glory walk
the stars
the start.

Dream   *I am lying on the beach with my face in the sand feeling the gritty pieces; I am rubbing my face in grief. Then I roll over and there he is, my father, as I have never seen him before. He is dressed completely in white, and his face is tan and relaxed, no lines or shades of gray. He bends down and puts his hand on my shoulder. He tells me he is happy being dead because he isn't sick anymore. He says that over and over, then leans back and is gone.*

sailor-man

mostly water is around us and lots of air and blue sky and
sun. the boat is bouncing around up and down like one of
those things you sit on at the park where the sister on the
other end sometimes goes flying if you push off too fast.
it's really a day that squeaks clean. my dad is yelling, "hard-
to-lee," and thwak, the boom comes over our heads, and
whoosh, the water flips up on deck when we all move to the
high side where it's safe. he smiles at us all sitting in a huddle
in the cockpit with our legs white from salt and sometimes
a cut from all the hurrying about. "grab the winch and wheel
her in," he tells my mom, and she turns on squeaky sneakers
to reach inside the cabin for the long metal bar that sticks
into a wheel on the side of the boat. she turns and pulls it
crinkcrank crinkcrank, crinkcrank, and the sail comes closer
like it is just going to wrap us up and take us with it, if it were
going anywhere, which it's not, just staying right here on
the boat where it belongs. in the center of the cockpit the
compass with a little spin-top in it moves all around with the
waves, up and down like something that could spill, but it
doesn't. my dad keeps looking at it, squinching up his white-
with-sun-stuff nose and trying to keep "on course," he says,
"so we don't end up in kingbucktoo or some such place."
he keeps pulling on the rudder, then he says, "come on over
here, kitty cat," taking my hand and plopping it on the smooth,
shiny handle that we poured smelly stuff on in the spring
to protect it from salt crudding up its skin. "now hold her
steady so i can go to the head," which is the bathroom on
the boat, not the thing on the top of our shoulders that we

use for thinking, and i say, "okay, dad," and jam my foot into the cockpit floor so i can make my body stiffer because hanging on to this thing is like riding those bucking broncos on tv except i am hanging on with two hands, like trying to make a tunnel for the tiller to live in so we don't go flopping about or get in some kind of trouble. mom just looks at me from the high side with her hair flying up in the back, and she tries to hold on with one hand and keep her hair down with the other but a huge wave comes and, "hold on," she shouts, grabbing my sister. in two shakes dad rockets out the hatch and is back. "here, dad, take over." but he says, "why don't you continue, you're doing so well." so there i am, sailing a family over the wild choppy blue water towards some cove where we're going to go swimming and have something special to eat.

usually we go to the boat on friday nights after everyone is finished with school and work and cleaning the house. we all travel in a big zigzag down a long road to spend the weekend on our boat named jezebel—"you always name a boat after a woman because you can never predict what she will do next." we all pile out of the station car with bunches of canvas and other slippery bags after making a million stops before finally getting here. it takes another million years just to get all the stuff from the car into the cart that we push down the wide-boarded dock. my dad pushes the cart because he is the biggest and the strongest, and he is good at not letting things get out of control. since the final dock is down below the place where the car is, the cart has to go downhill quite a bit before stopping, and so he has to pull on it very hard to keep it from slamming through all the railings and plopping into the drink. his wide back gets all bulked up, and the veins in his arms plump up like little worms in the dirt.

we load our stuff into the launch, and finally we are underway, with the launch guy pushing the rudder back and forth as he takes us out to our boat. the wind is flapping all the way, and the boats kick back and forth like toys instead of places where real life happens. our boat is way out. sometimes when we arrive at the dock and scan the horizon with our hands to see if she is still there, we miss her, and what a feeling that is, like something huge is lost in the night. then we always see her, bobbing away on the mooring like a wild horse waiting for us to ride her.

as soon as we're on board, mom cooks the boat dinner of meat, corn, and potatoes all fried up in the pan that smells like a restaurant. for dessert she brings out chocolate pudding in a can, and daddy claps his hands just one time in the glee he is experiencing from such joy. he loves chocolate pudding and just about anything chocolate. anytime we go out to dinner, he always asks for chocolate ice cream for dessert, "with oodles and oodles of chocolate sauce, please." that oodles and oodles always makes the waitress smile and tilt her head, like what a strange tall man wanting chocolate sauce, shouldn't the kids be wanting that, which we probably are, except not oodles and oodles, just a regular amount.

after dinner it's time to buckle down the hatches and get everything stored away so that it won't slide all over the place when the sailing starts tomorrow. my dad is up on deck, tying things down, pushing a rag with smelly stuff over the wood, but mostly he is just soaking up the salty air. being on the water on this boat that he loves gives him a new life.

when bedtime rolls around, everyone loads up into their beds for sleeping, and there is some carrying on from me and my two sisters. since the boat isn't supposed to be where you live your whole life, it is kind of small "down below, not stairs, don't say downstairs," he always says. my two sisters and i sleep in the main cabin, and mom and dad sleep up front, their bodies looking like a bow. their heads and arms are apart, but their feet come together in a vee that looks like they are heading in the right direction. we all clamber about, giggling and pushing, up on the bunk above, and daddy, who is never really in bed, flaps a big finger our way and tells us, "shush up," but not like he really means it or anything because he doesn't care really what goes on, he is just so happy to be here. the rest of the world can fall apart for all he cares. then he leans down and gets a bucket to begin scooping water out of places where it shouldn't be.

after a while he moves into the cabin with his top shirt off and a cigarette in his mouth, lit but not really burning yet. he sees my sister on the top bunk, gives her a tickle on her stomach, then throws a big hand my way, "okay now, slow it down with all the noise a bit." then he picks up my other sister's bear that has fallen out of bed and throws it at her head, making her "ohhh" and "wheee" and kick her feet. then we try to go to sleep, and daddy heads back up on deck to check on everything. he lifts the boards that keep us from wandering up

on deck at night and falling into the water, then pushes that
huge body up towards the sky.

from where i lie, i see him there in the dark, the puff of the
cigarette going from a lot of red to a little bit. sometimes i
can't see his face at all, just the line around him like he has
no face, which i know is just ridiculous because everyone
has a face; it's something god gives us when we are born.

one night we're all sitting on the edge of the boat writing in
the water with our toes, waiting for mom to put dinner on
the brown table that pulls away from the wall. all of a sudden
there is a big racket from down below, like something awful is
going on. smoke and flames start flying all around, tall ones
that mean this is bad news. mom is screaming something that
doesn't matter because we get the message with the flames.
dad takes one giant step from where he is sitting in the back
of the boat and goes down below. he picks up the stove,
which is on fire, with both hands, like he is holding a tray of
something at a party, would you like one, and he hurls himself
up the little stairs back onto the deck. the flames are dancing
about, and i think for a minute that maybe they will go out just
being on deck, maybe the air will put them out, but they race
higher. he looks around from side to side, which isn't hard to
do since the boat isn't very wide, and then he just puffs up
his cheeks with more air than usual and tosses the stove into
the water, just throws it in there like something that might go
flying out a window in an argument, only no one is angry here,
just not wanting the world to burn up. there is a splash that
makes me stand up because whenever you hear a splash on

the boat it means something has fallen overboard and might need immediate rescuing. the stove bobs there for a minute, like it might float and save itself, a little metal barge that might be going somewhere. i want to save it on principle because nothing should be left to sink to the bottom, but there is nothing else to do; the stove is finished.

it floats for a minute, and the fire starts to go out with a hiss. then the stove twists in on itself and starts rocking back and forth, each time getting a little deeper as it goes, until with a heavy glubbing it just slides down the drain, a watery, silver smudge that gets farther and farther away until we can't see anything anymore except green eternity. then my dad claps his hands together; he always does this, as if he is going to make some speech like the president of the united states or just like my dad who is very important, and then we have dinner from a can, a family that is saved by a happy sailor.

Epilogue

There isn't a day that passes that he isn't with me, all around me. Sometimes I smell him when I am in line at the bank or driving down the long road home. He comes to me in a sense that I can take, not in a surprise that scares me. I used to think I wanted him to appear to me at night, just come and sit down on the bed as he would do if he were really here. I wanted him to know that he could come if he wanted to. But someone told me that if we constantly want the dead around us, we keep them from passing into new life. While it is still hard for me to imagine that my father is really dead, I have stopped asking him to come. Now I just see him in the leaves on the trees and hear his voice in the wind at night.

Many years in the future, if people look hard enough, I am sure they will find a fossil of my father in the layers of my life.

REFERENCES

The Book of Common Prayer and Administration of the Sacraments and Other Rites and Ceremonies of the Church. New York: Seabury Press, 1953.

Frankl, Viktor E. *The Unheard Cry for Meaning: Psychotherapy and Humanism.* New York: Simon and Schuster, 1978.

International Graphic Society. *Life and Its Marvels: Plant, Animal, Human.* Englewood Cliffs, N.J.: Esco Publishing Company, 1960.

Jensen, Adolf. "Murmuring Zephyrs." In *Masterpieces of Piano Music.* Edited by Albert E. Wier. New York: Mumil Publishing Company, 1918.

Jensen, Mari N. "Ancient Fish in Decline." *ABC News Science* (April 1999): http://abcnews.go.com/sections/science/DailyNews/fish980819.html

Oliver, Mary. "Wild Geese." *Dream Work.* New York: The Atlantic Monthly Press, 1986.

Walker, Alice. "How Poems Are Made / A Discredited View." *Literature and Its Writers: An Introduction to Fiction, Poetry, and Drama.* Eds. Ann Charters and Samuel Charters. Boston: Bedford Books, 1997.

ACKNOWLEDGMENTS

Many people helped me in the process of writing and publishing this book. Thanks to the New York Foundation for the Arts for its financial support. To my colleagues in the MCC English Department for their continued encouragement. To Judith Kitchen, M. Garrett Bauman, and Robert Herzog for their willingness to read the galleys, especially during the busiest time of the semester, and for their gracious reviews. To Debbie Mohr in the MCC library for her gracious assistance in locating out-of-date publishers and sources. To my piano teacher, Jennifer Undercofler, whose explanations of a barrio lead me to a deeper understanding between disease and memory. To my publisher, VanderWyk & Burnham, for believing in the book. To Jean A. McDonough, whose remarkable talent and intuition pulled the fragments of the book together into something beyond my design.

And to my mother and sisters for their willingness to relive many, many difficult moments as we remembered the joys and sorrows of my father's life.